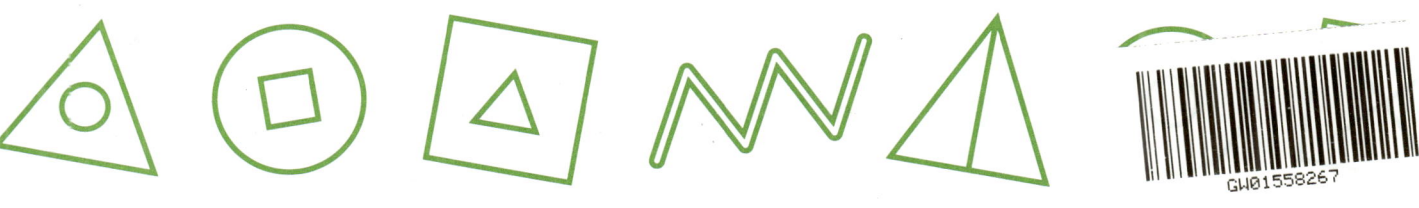

· JENNY ACKLAND ·

At Home with Pattern and Shape

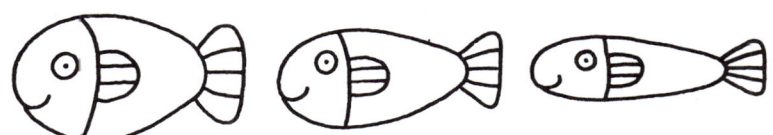

· Oxford University Press ·

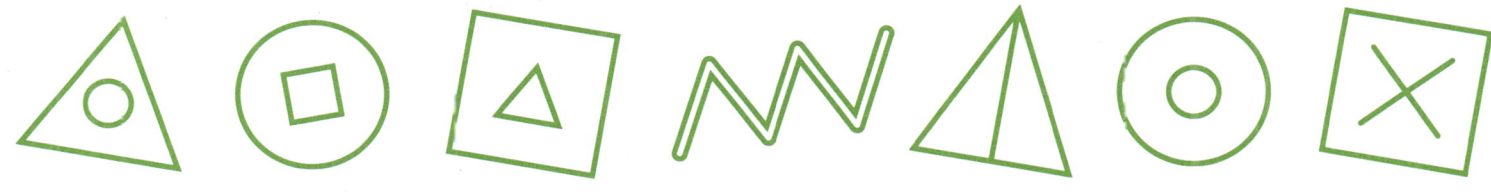

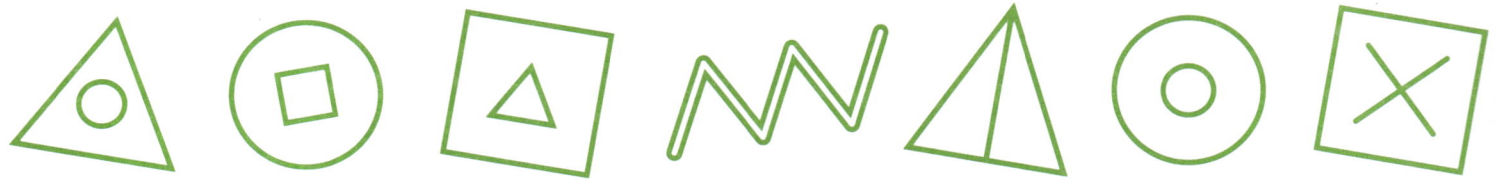

How to help your child

- Choose a quiet time to sit together, when your child is not tired or distracted.
- Work in short periods of activity, and stop as soon as your child loses concentration.
- Talk through the activities with your child, so that he or she develops the language to describe shapes, and patterns, and size.
- Apply these descriptions to objects around the home, so that your child realizes that mathematics is very much a part of everyday life.
- Give plenty of praise and encouragement.
- Remember that the workbook should be fun for your child, as well as being educationally worthwhile.

About Pattern and Shape

This workbook continues from *At Home with Shape and Size*.

The process of learning about patterns, and shapes, and size involves all of the following skills:

- visual discrimination between different patterns, shapes, and sizes
- hand–eye coordination in filling in patterns
- recognition and prediction of continuing patterns and sequences
- three-dimensional awareness, of shape in space
- developing a vocabulary to describe shape and size
- estimation of differences in dimensions
- early measurement

Further notes on the individual sections are provided on page 48.

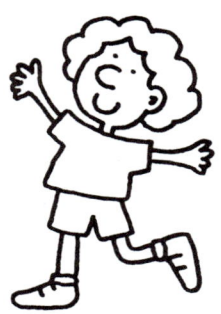

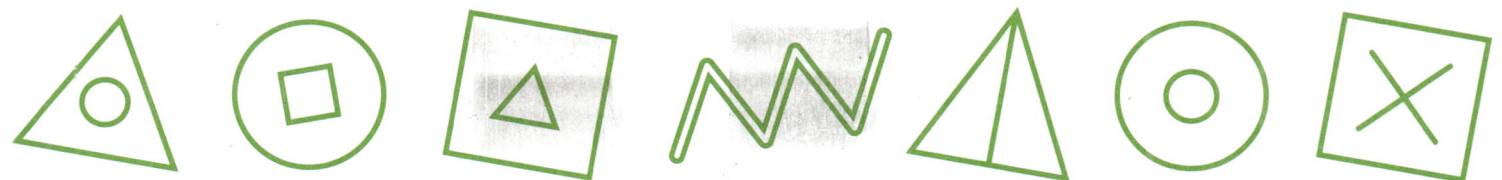

• CONTENTS •

Join the same 4–9

Find more the same 10–13

Make the same 14–25

Find the shape 26–31

Same size 32–33

Biggest and smallest 34–37

Patterns 38–41

What comes next? 42–47

Notes for parents 48

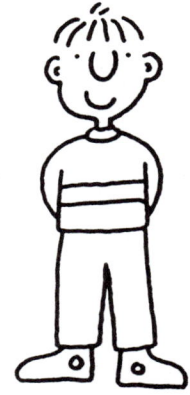

Join up the same

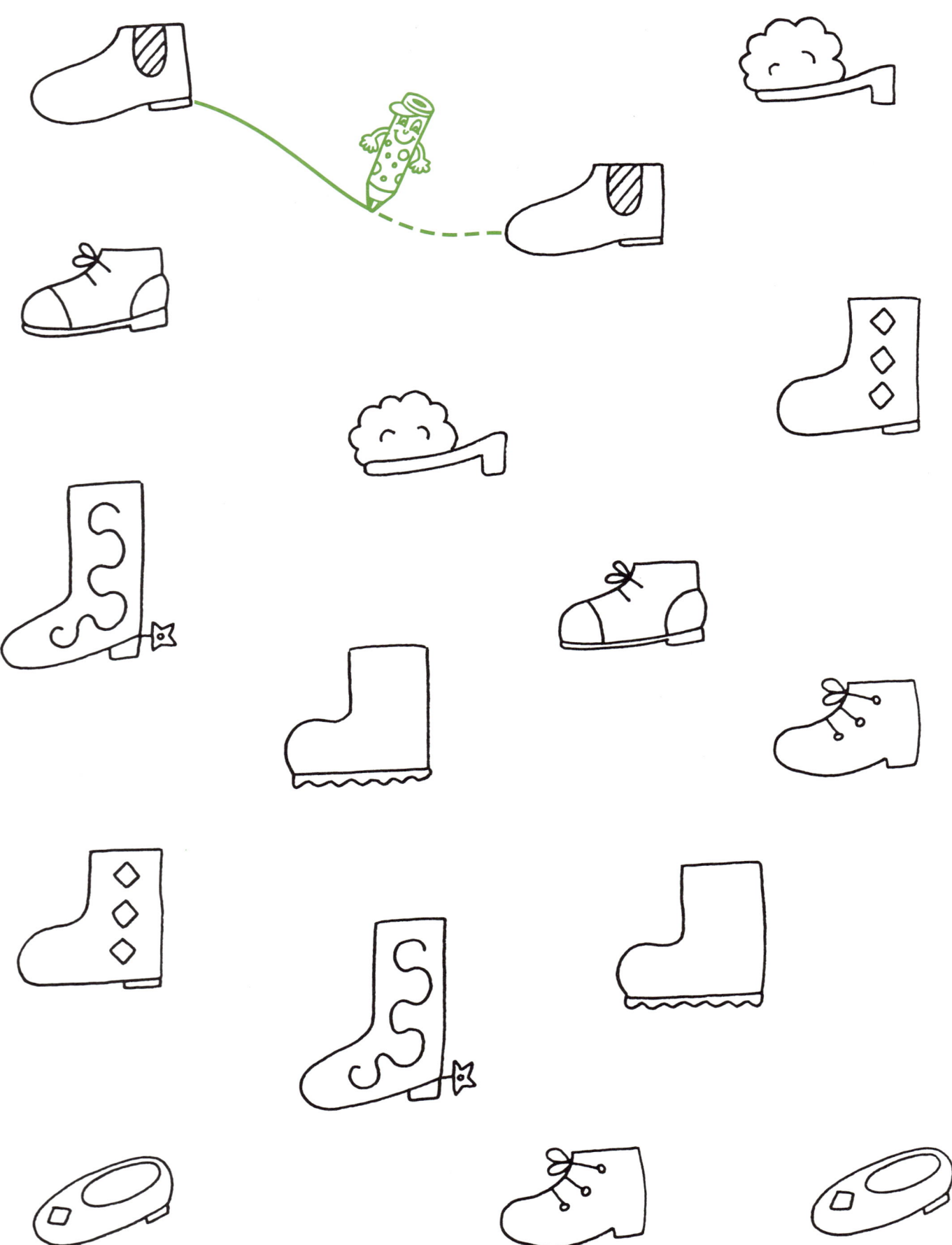

Join up the same

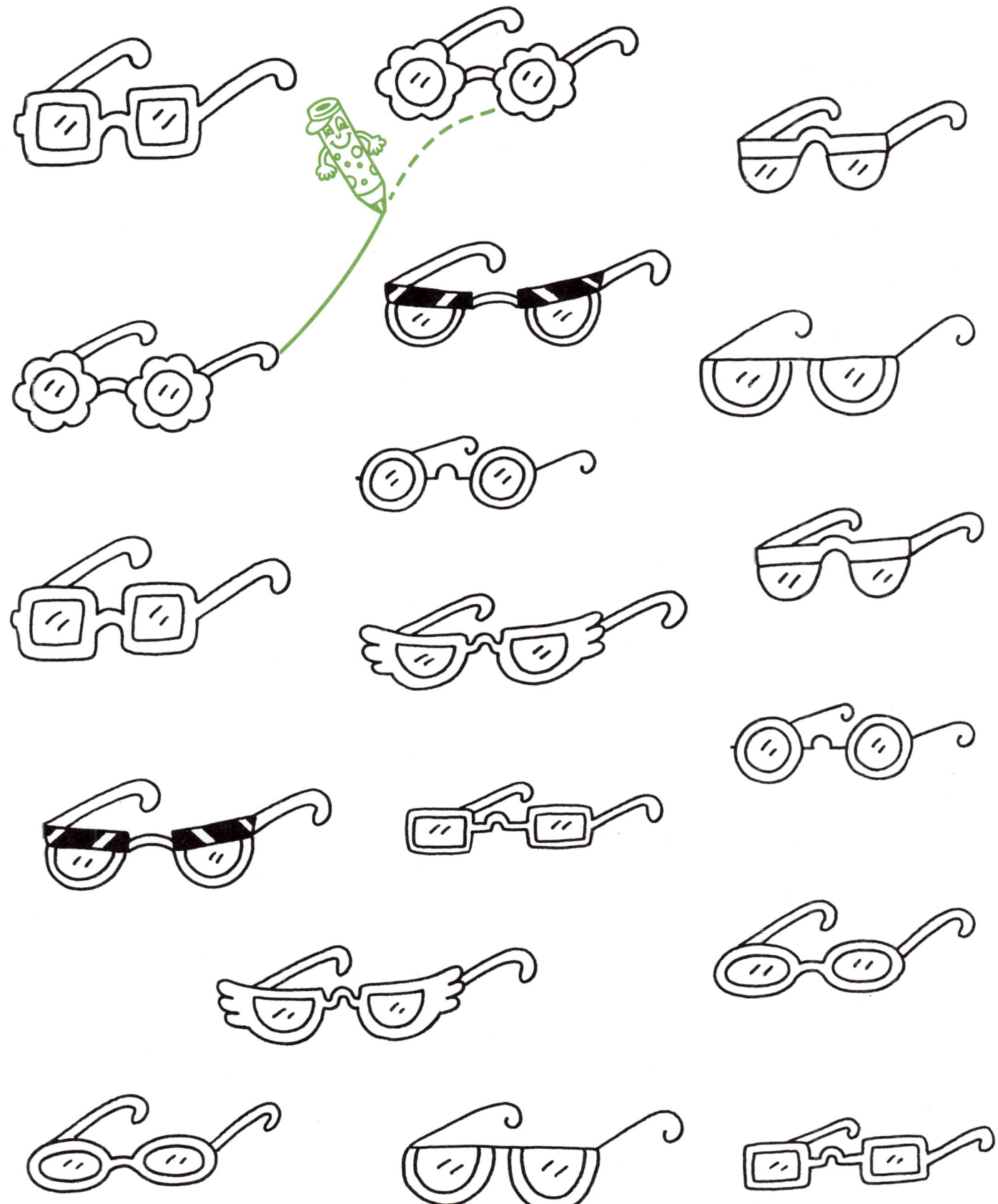

Join up the same

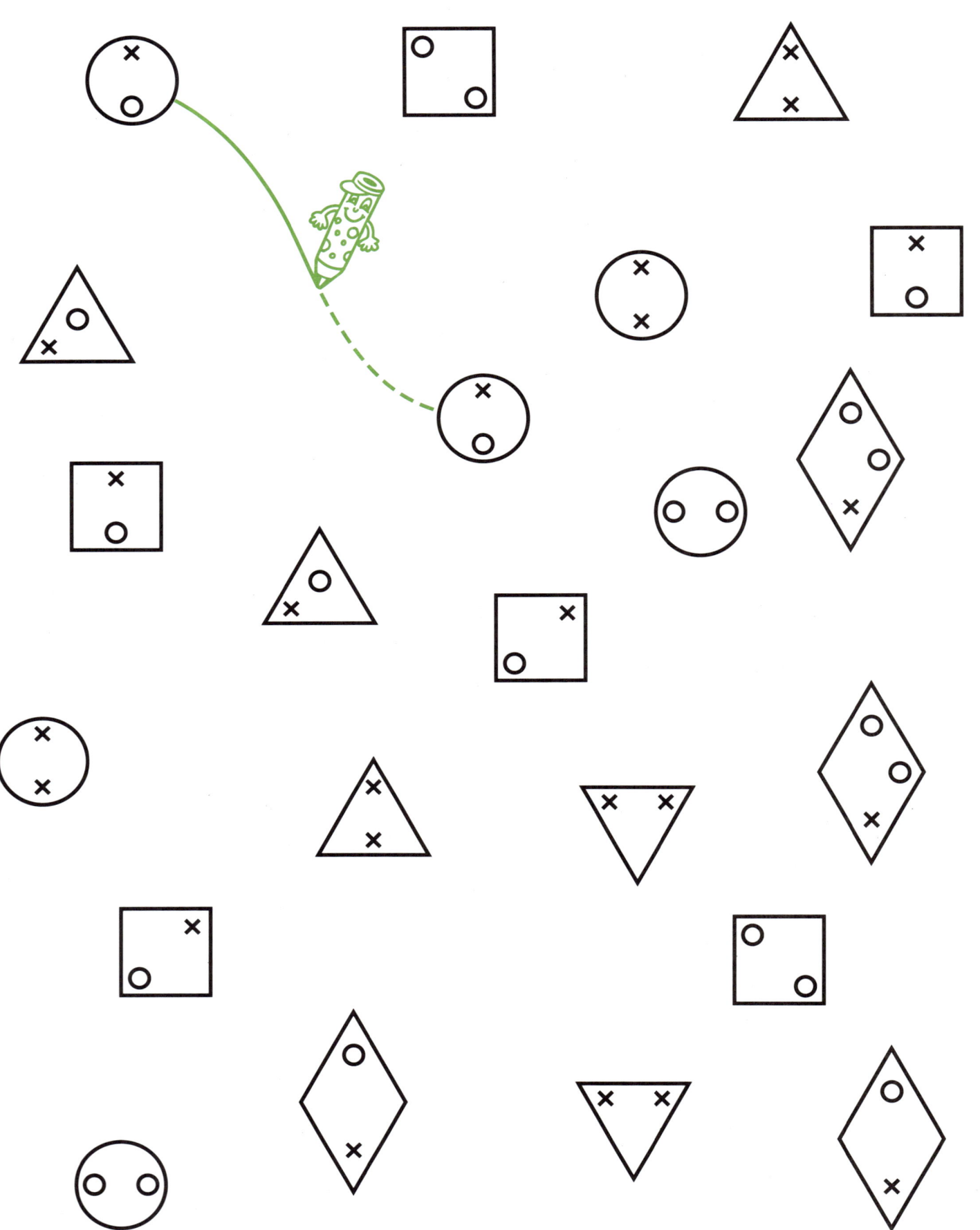

Join up the same

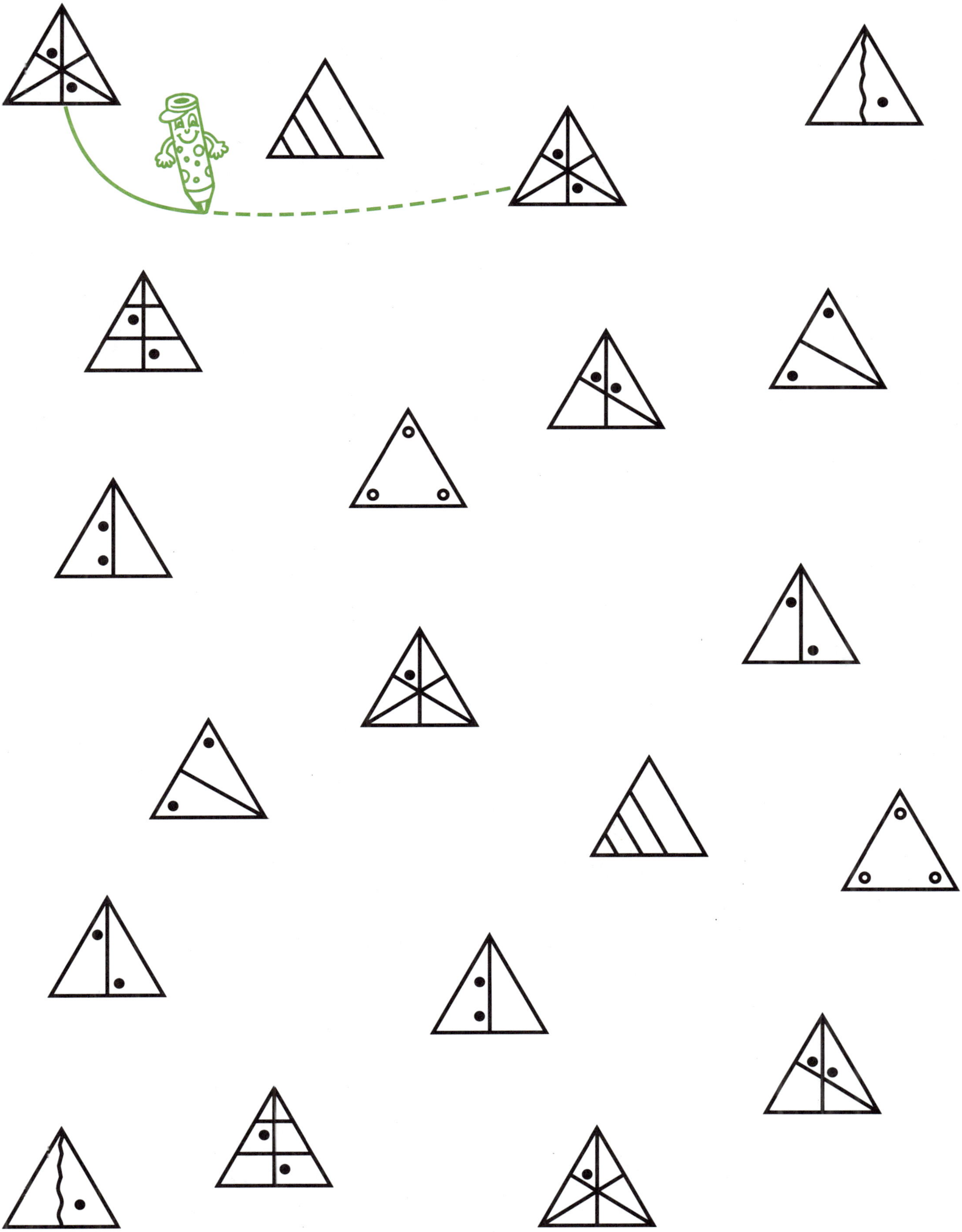

Join up the same pattern
Colour the same colour

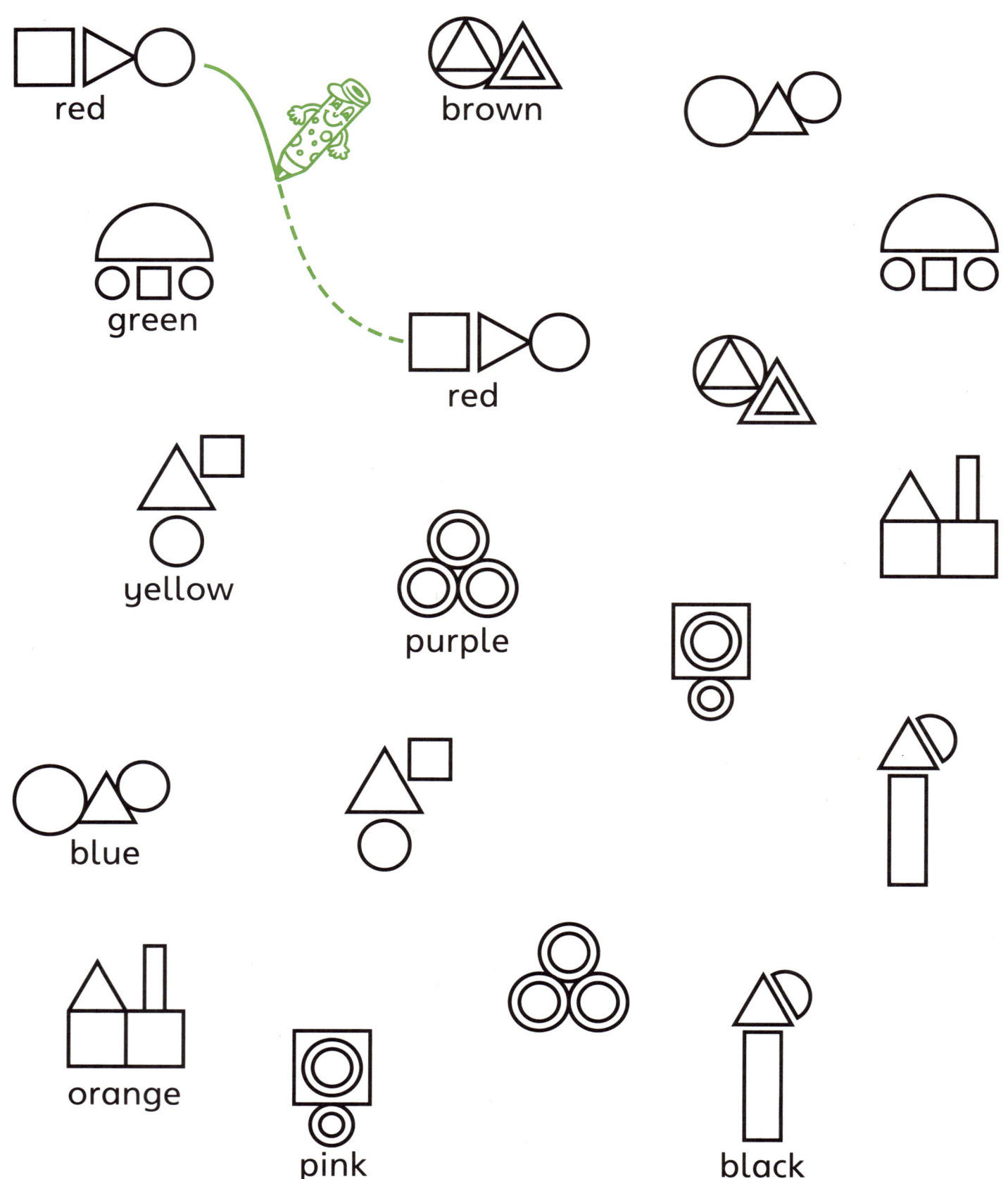

Join up the same shape
Colour the same colour

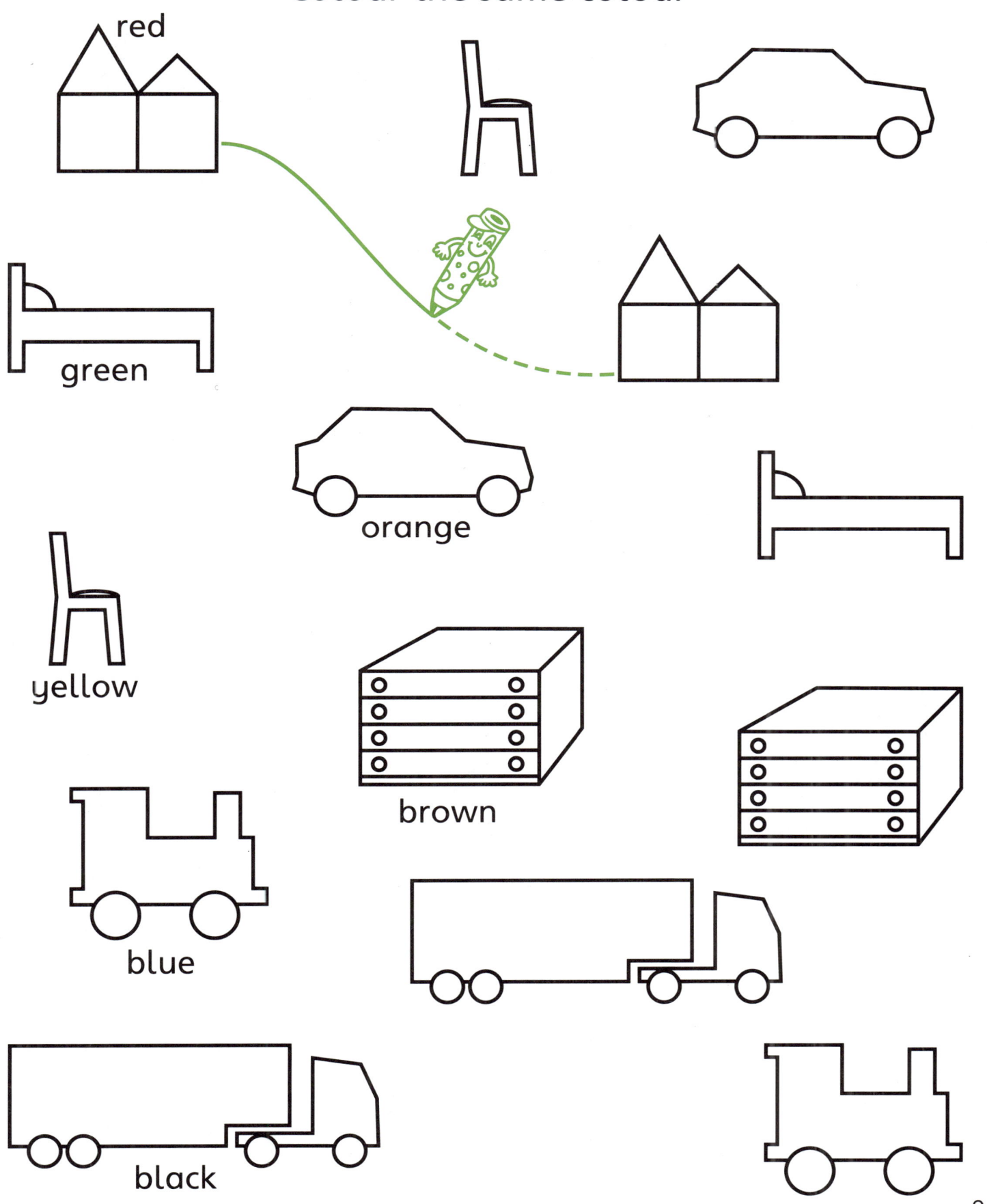

Find 3 more the same

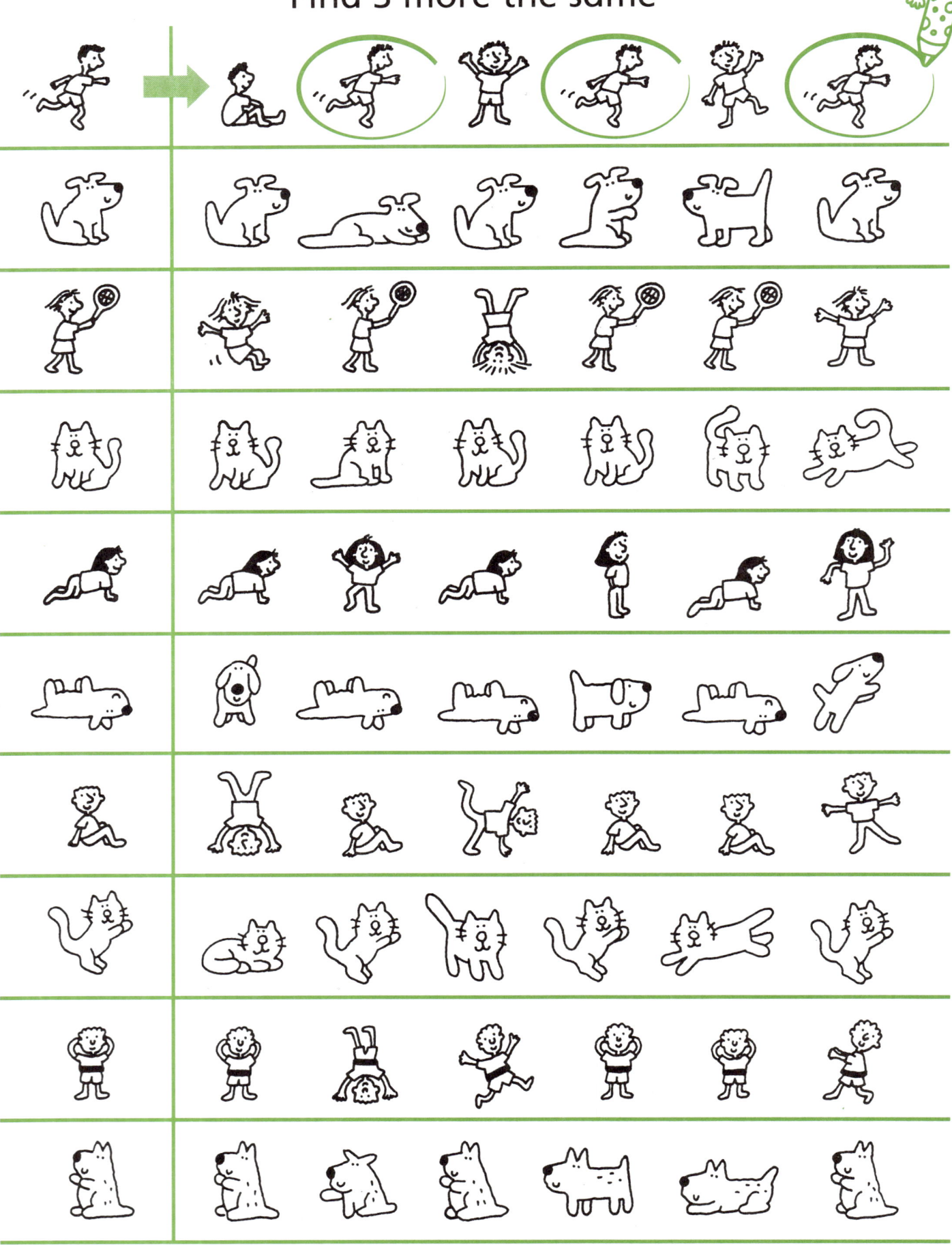

Find 3 more the same

Find 3 more the same

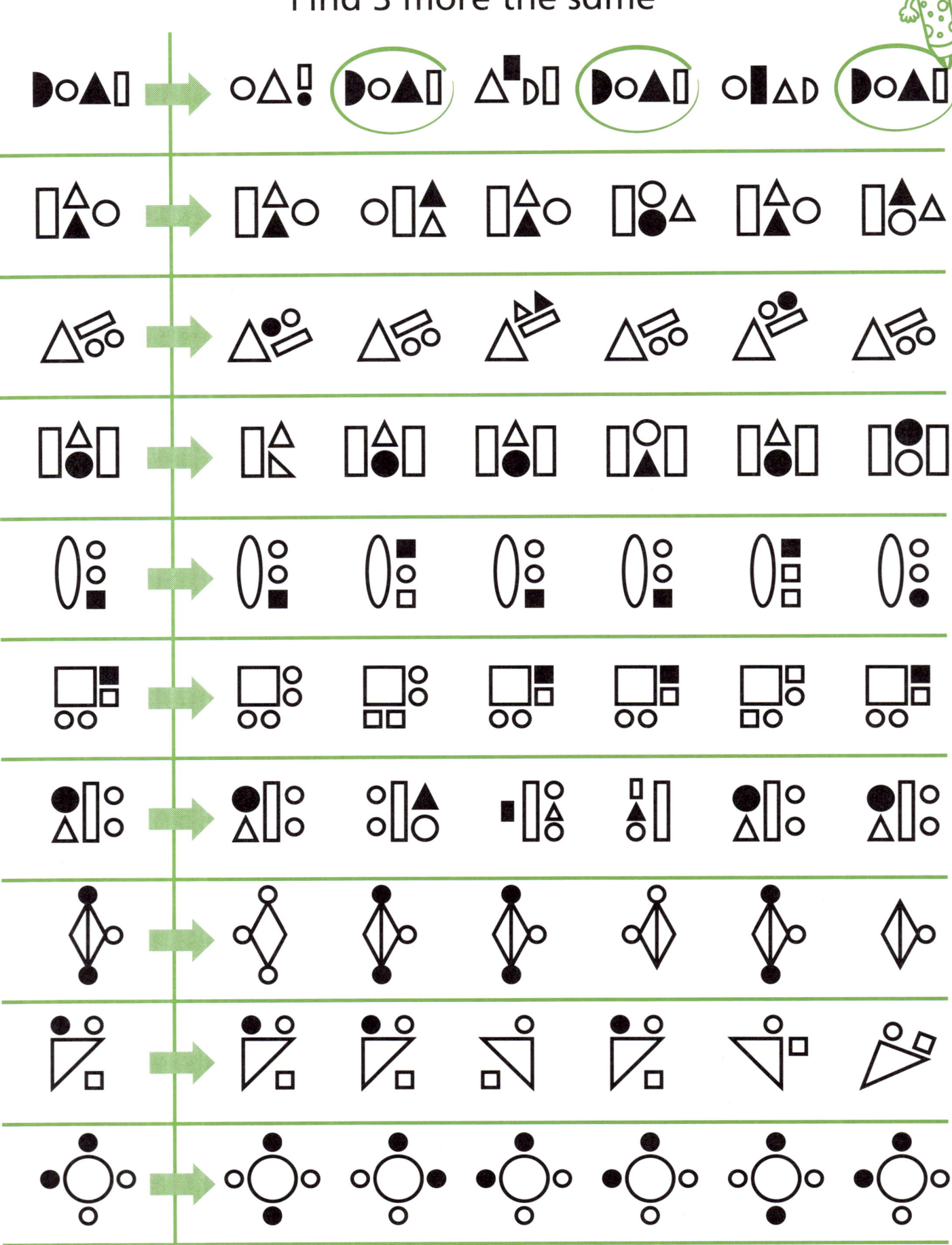

Find 3 more the same. Colour the same colour

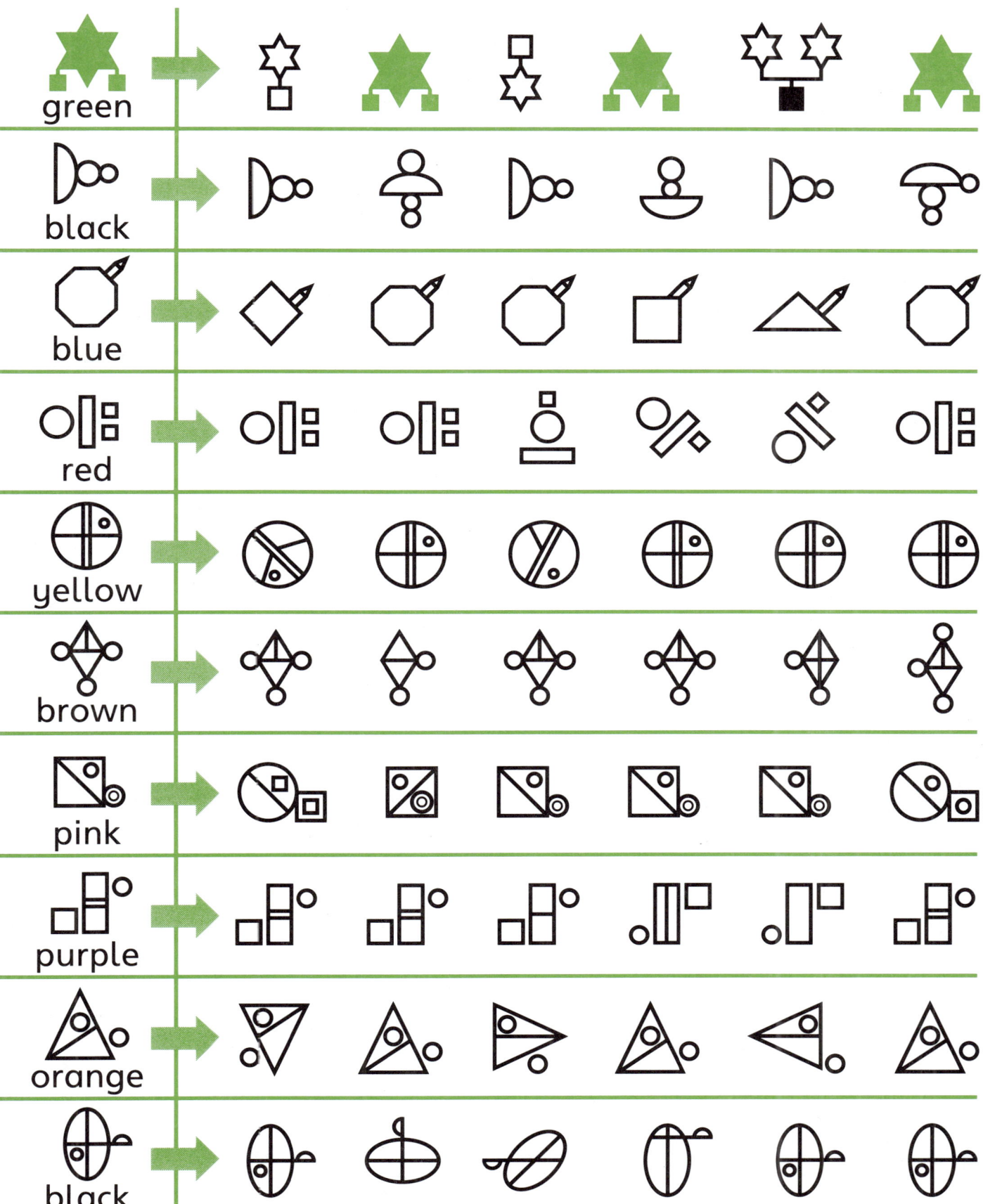

Make the same

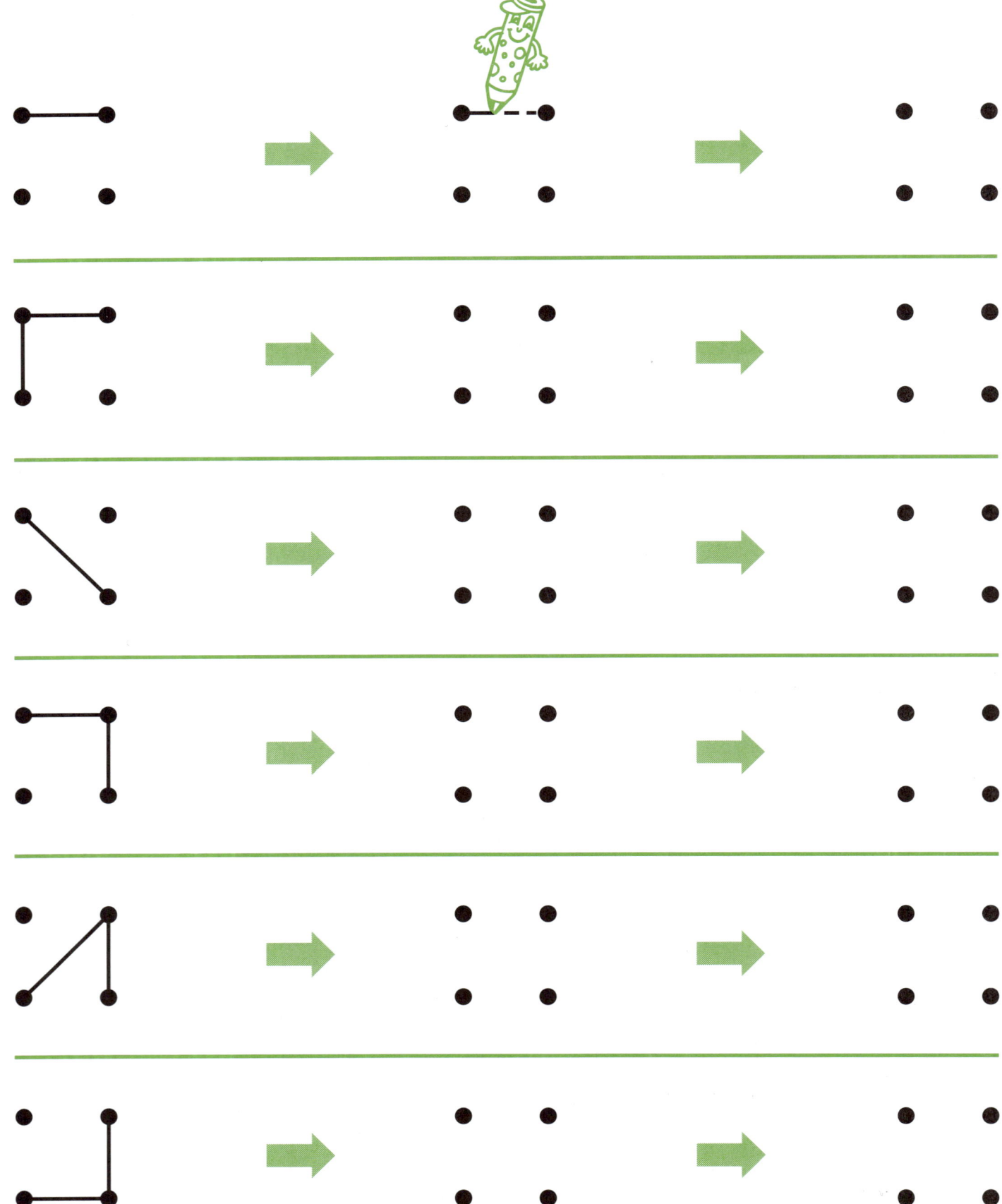

Make the same

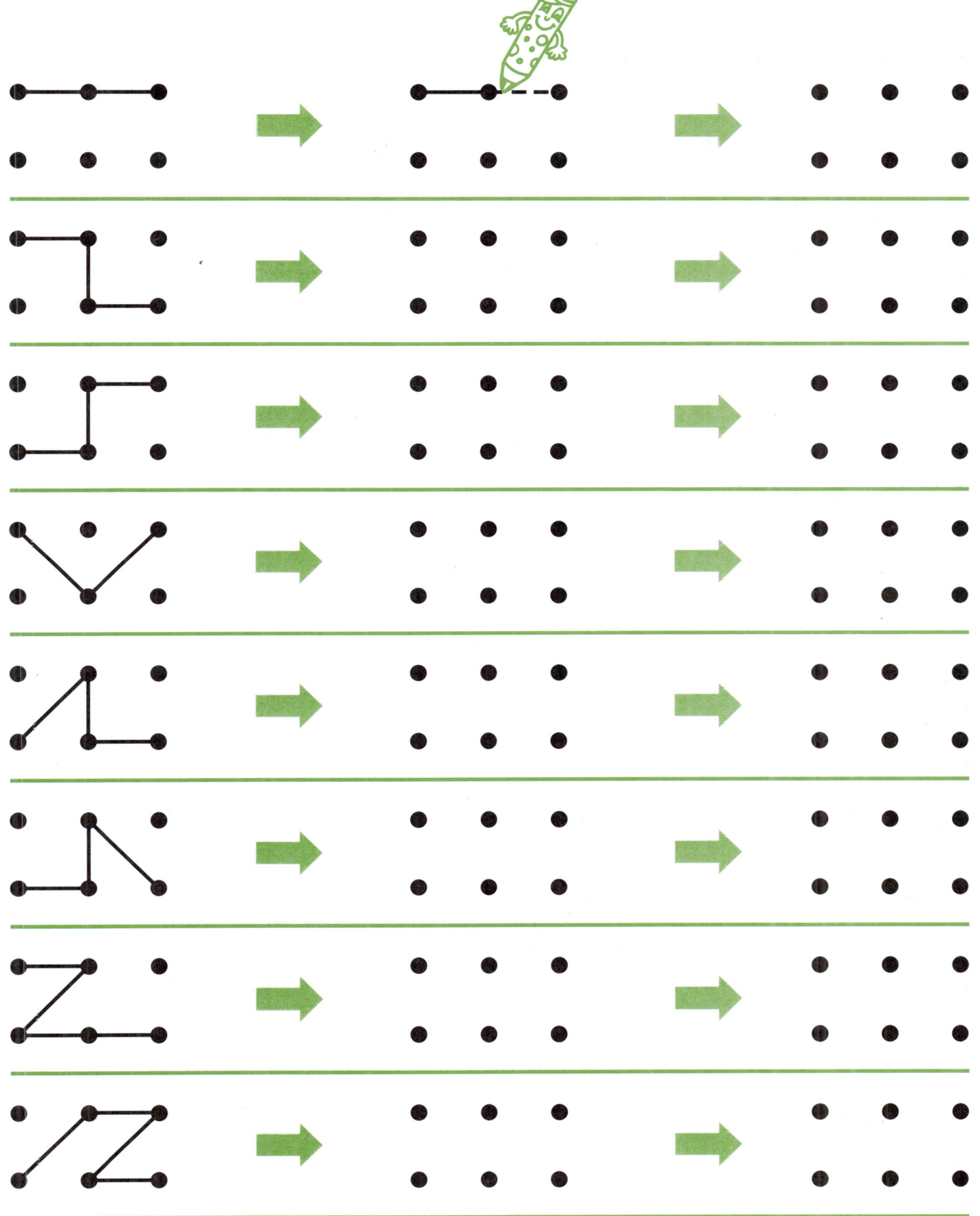

15

Make the same

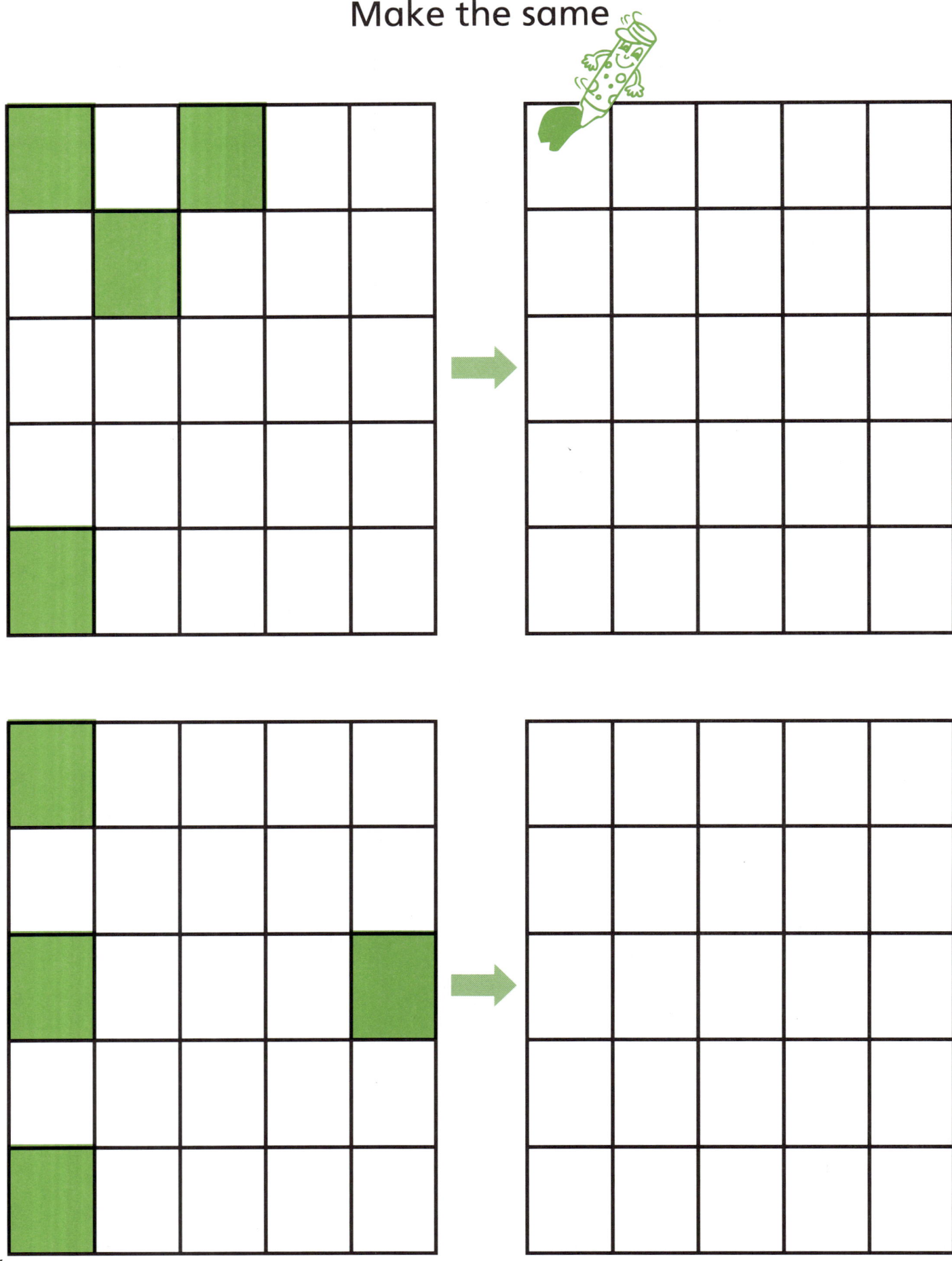

Make the same

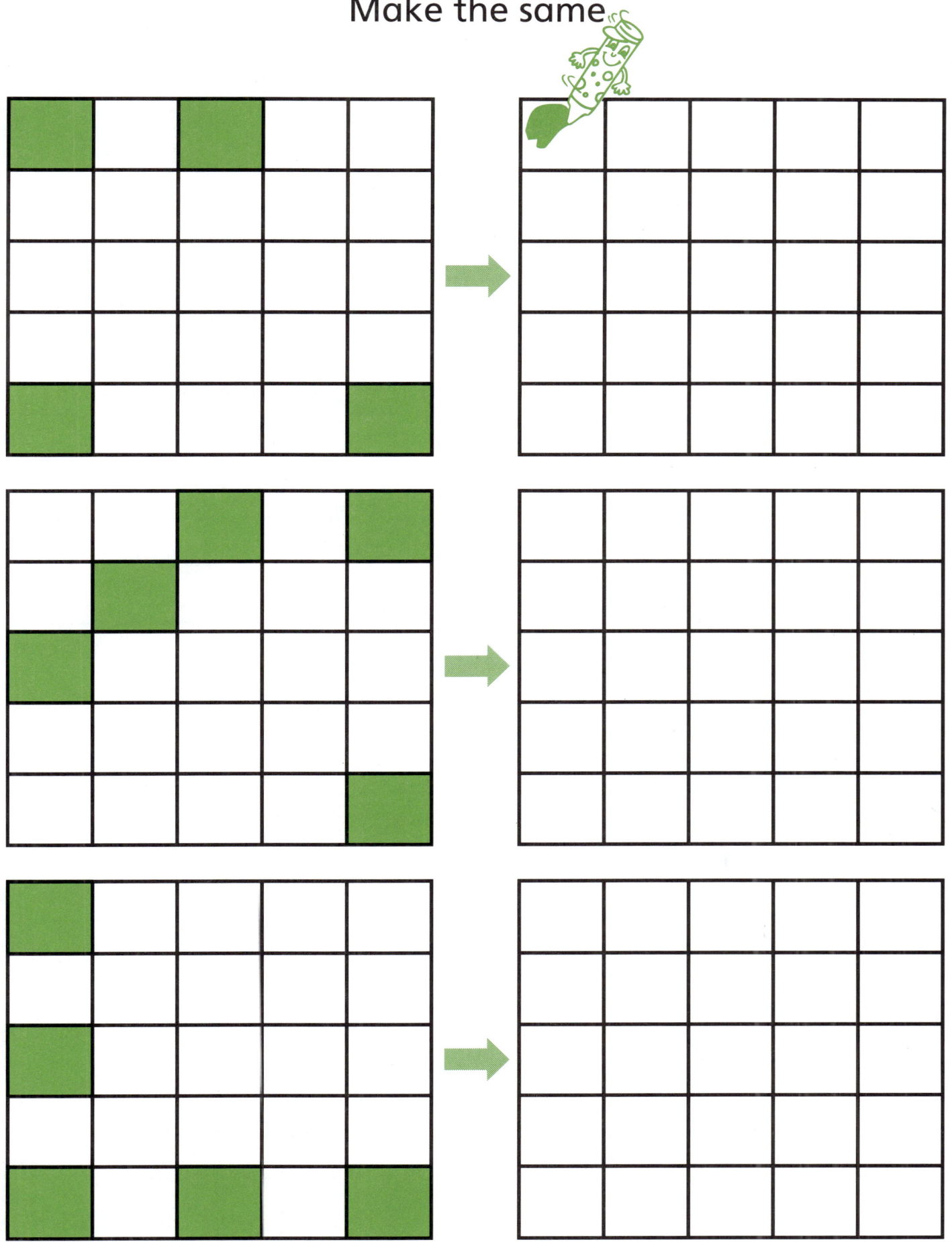

Make the same

1 = red   2 = blue   3 = green   4 = yellow

Make the same

1 = brown   2 = orange   3 = purple   4 = pink   5 = black

Make the same

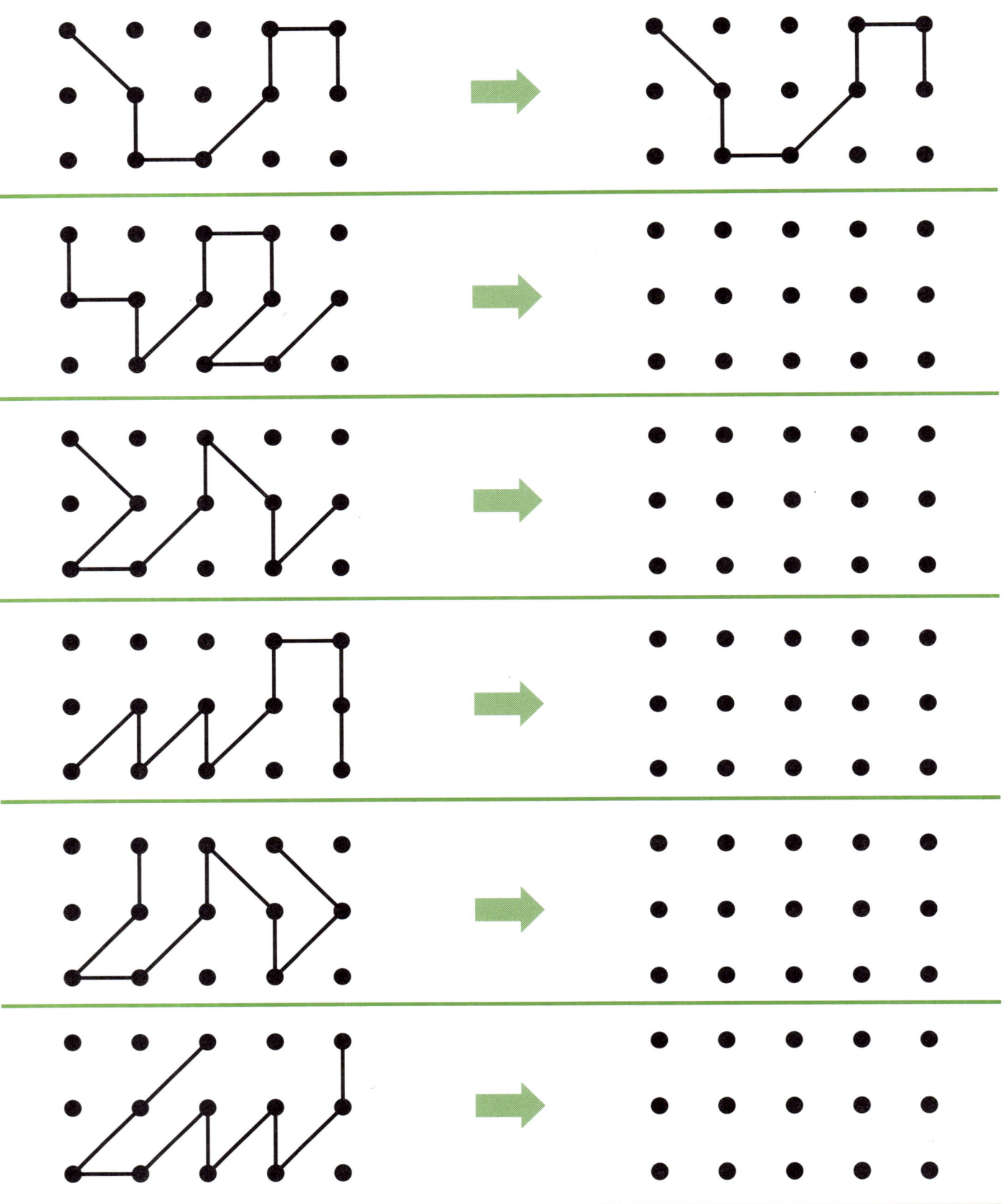

Make the same

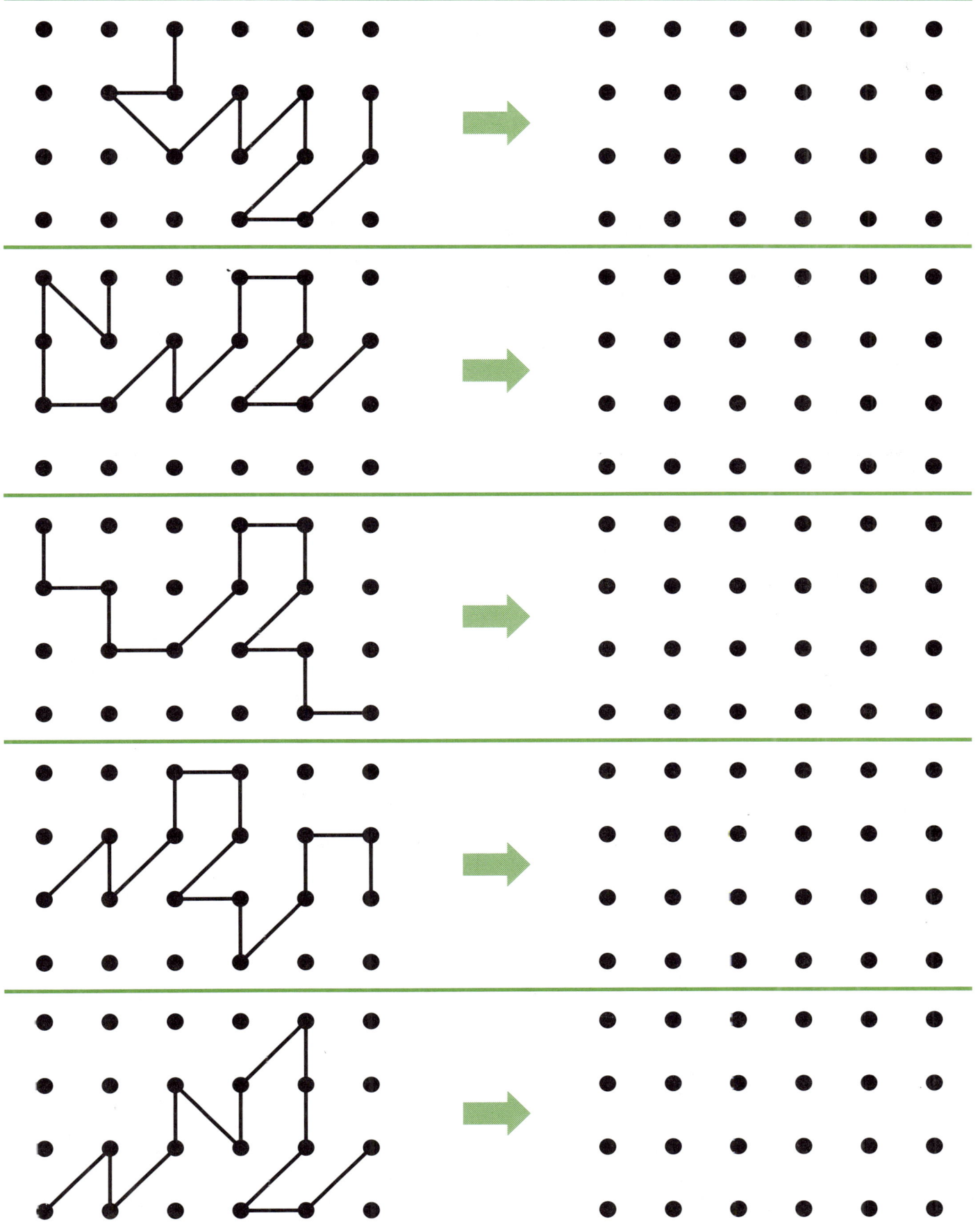

# Make the same colour
r=red   b=blue   g=green   y=yellow

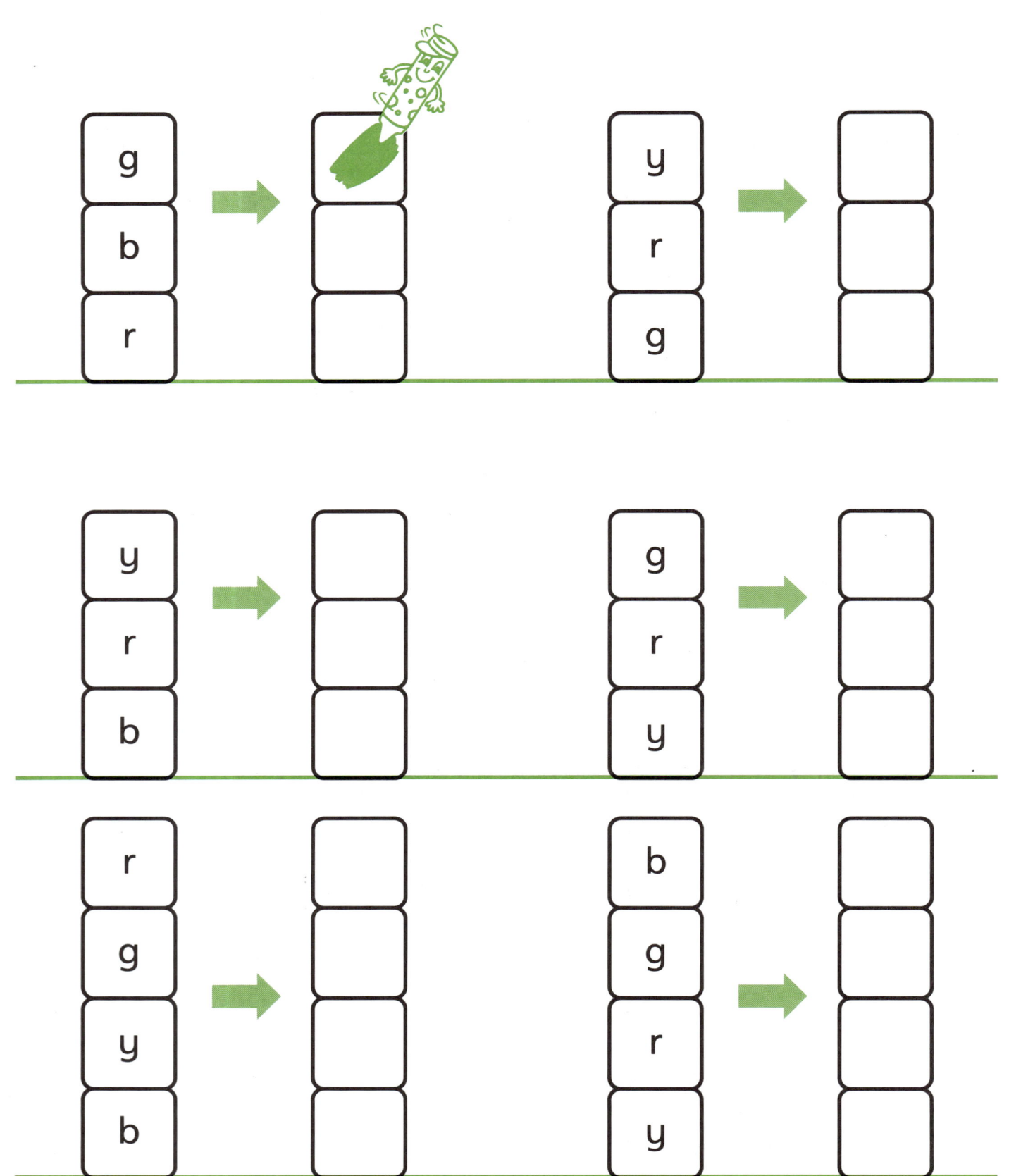

# Make the same colour
r=red   b=blue   g=green   y=yellow

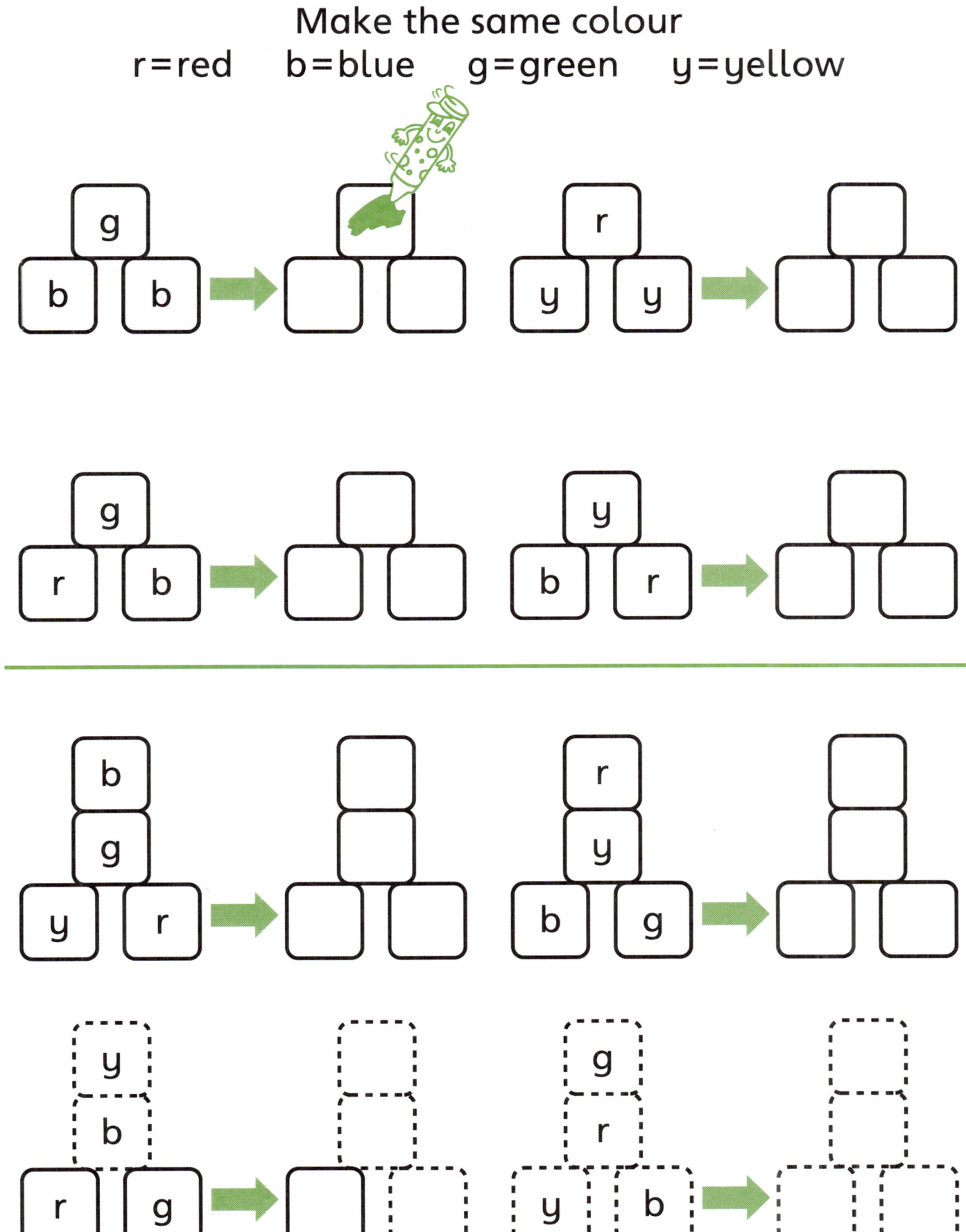

Make the same colour

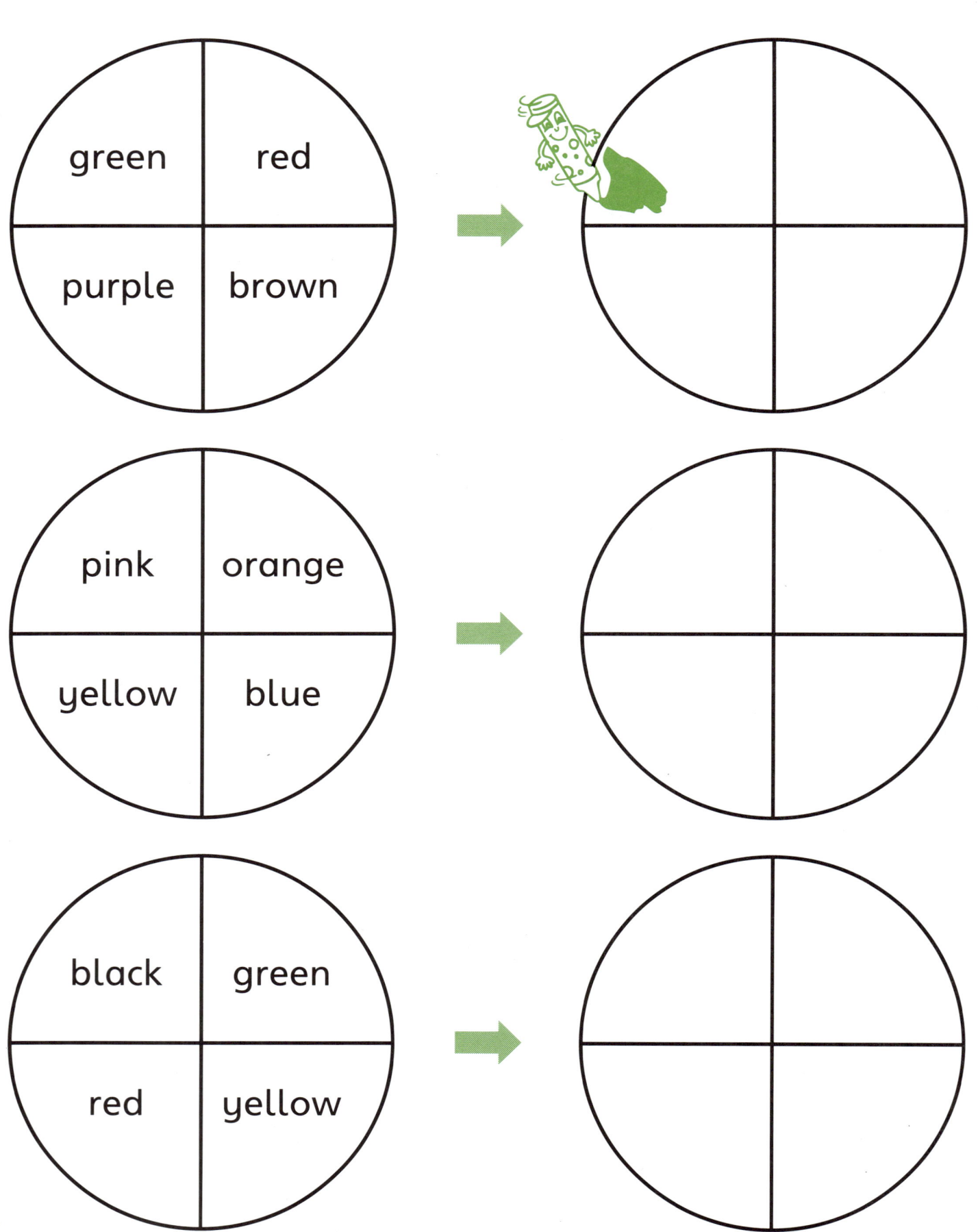

Make the same pattern

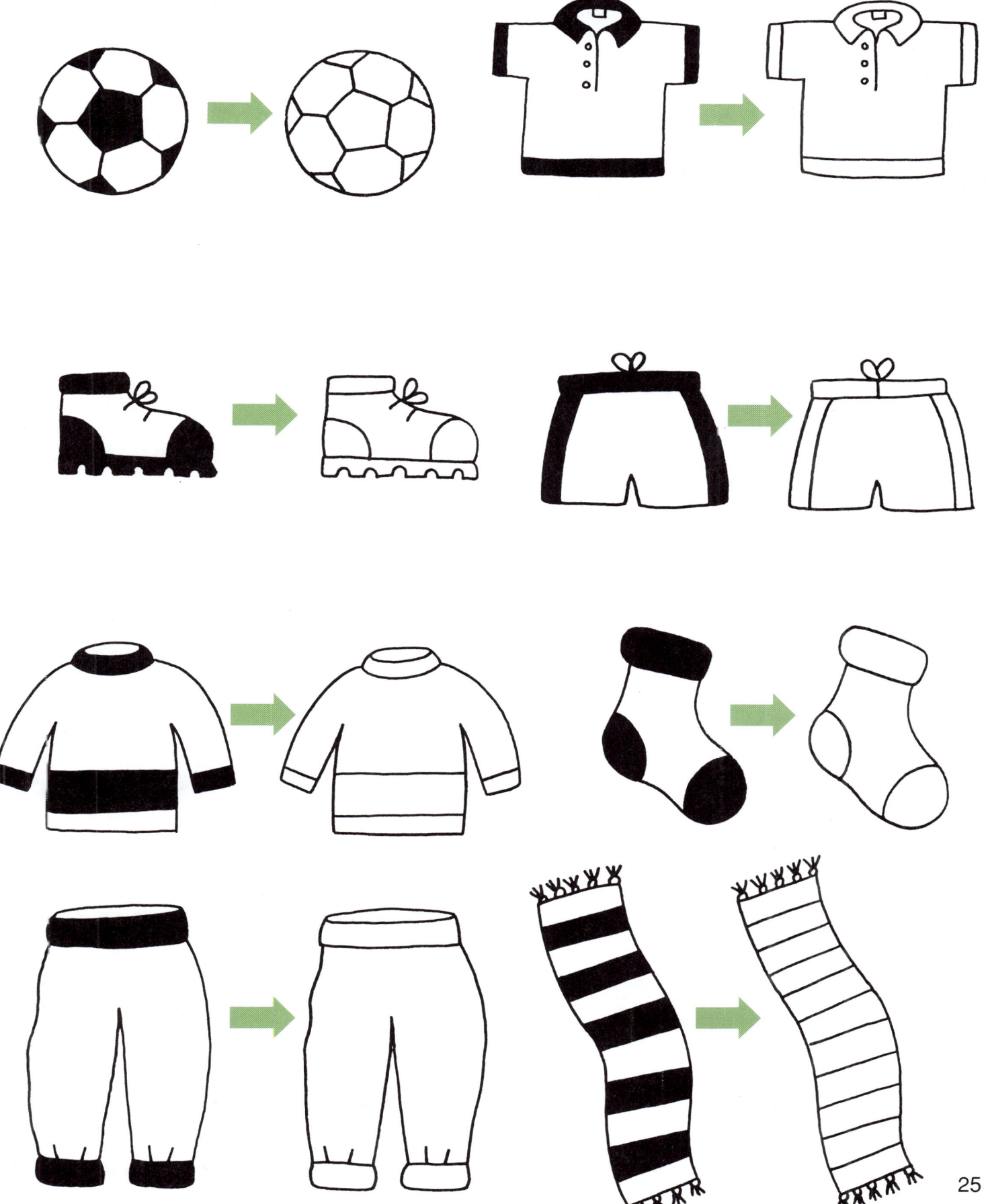

Find the same shape

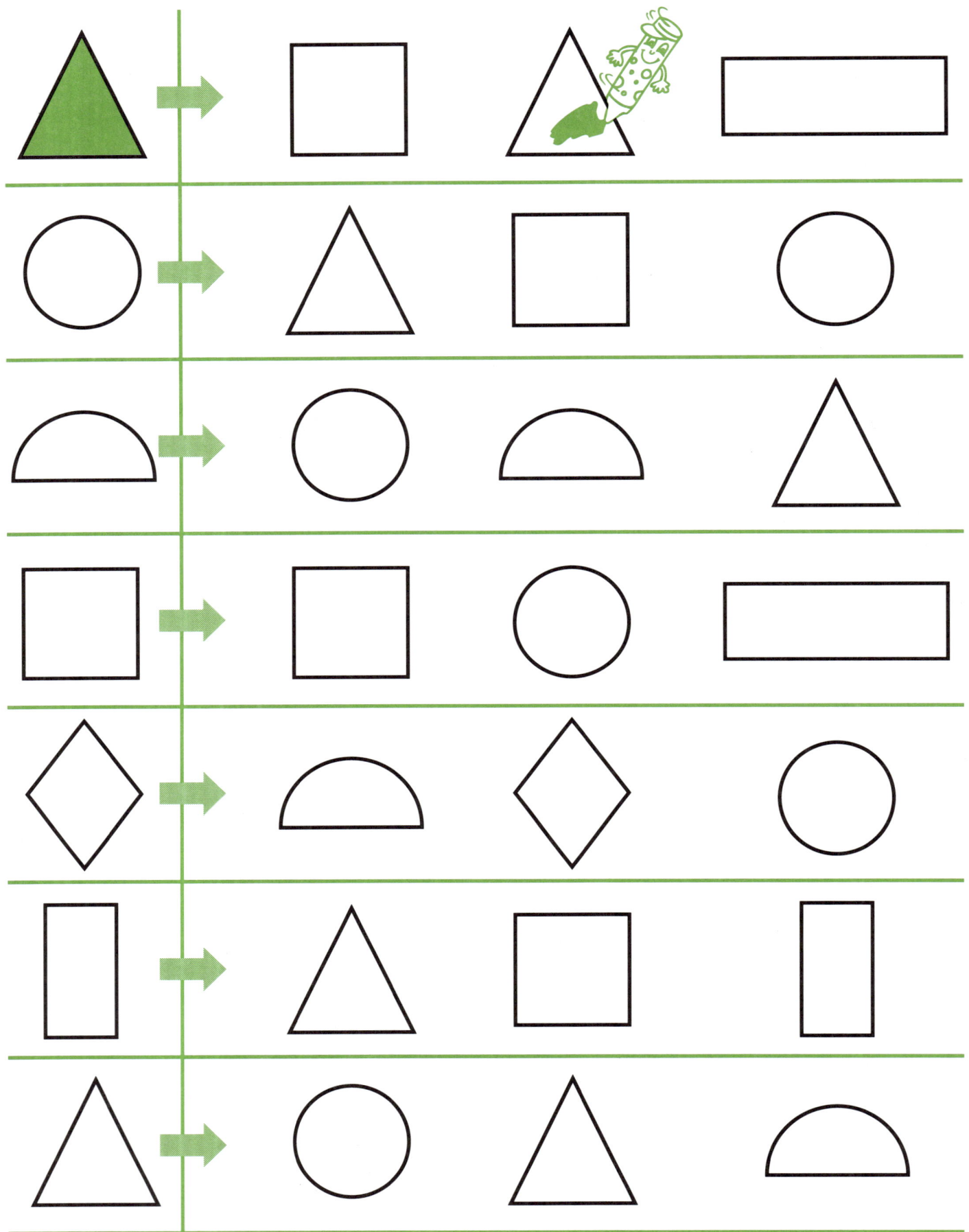

Find the shapes

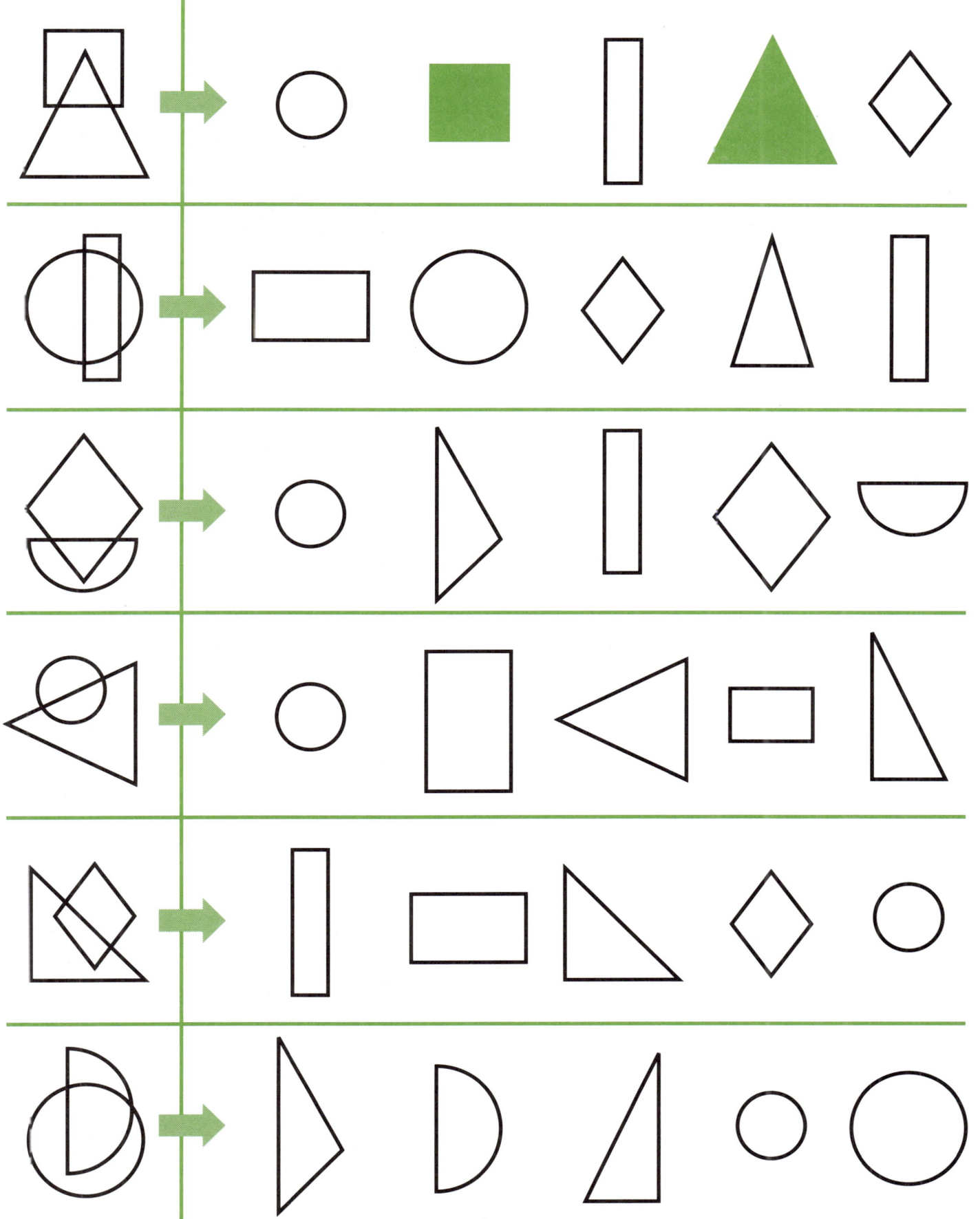

Find the shape

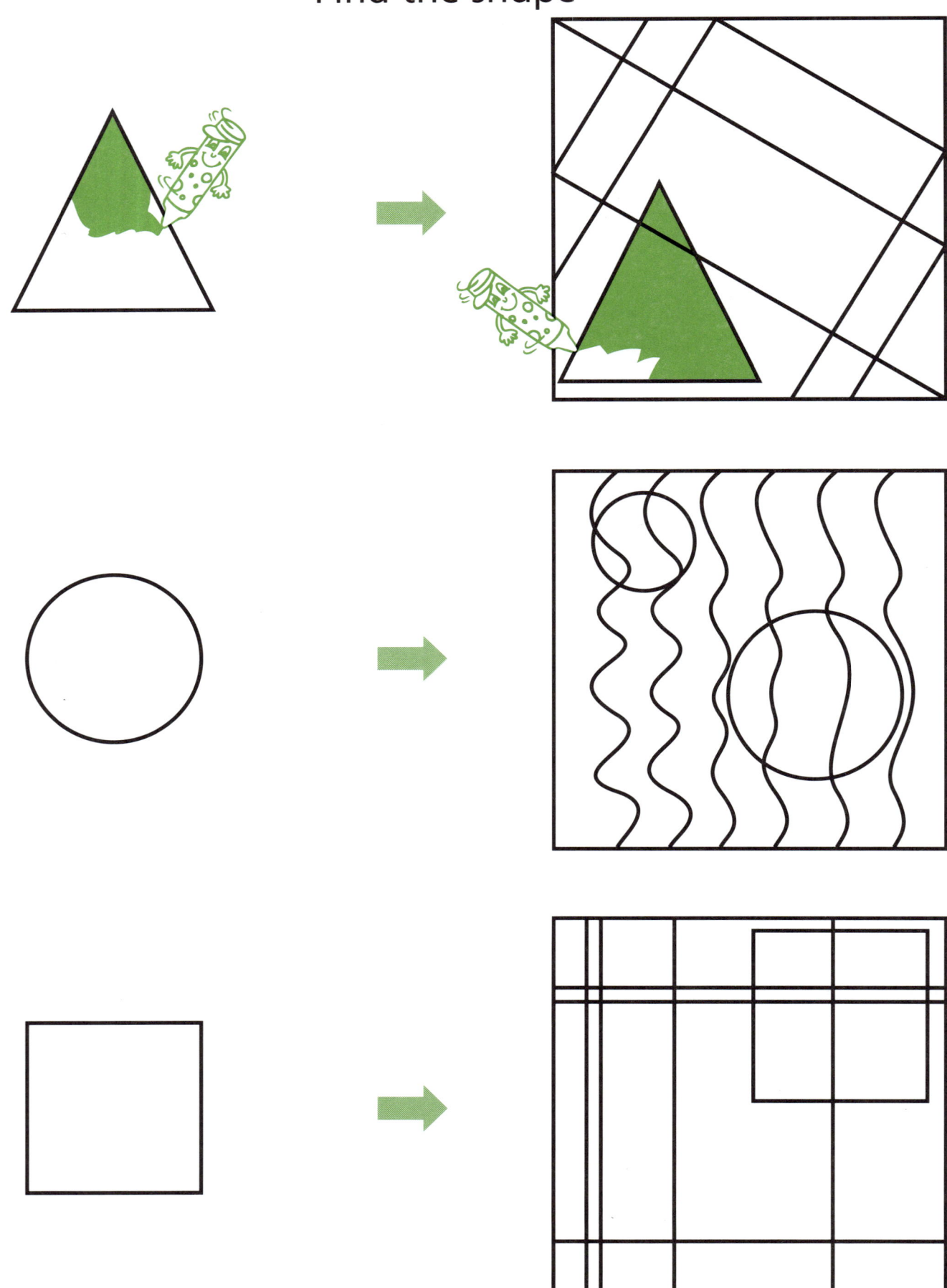

Find the shapes
Colour the same colour

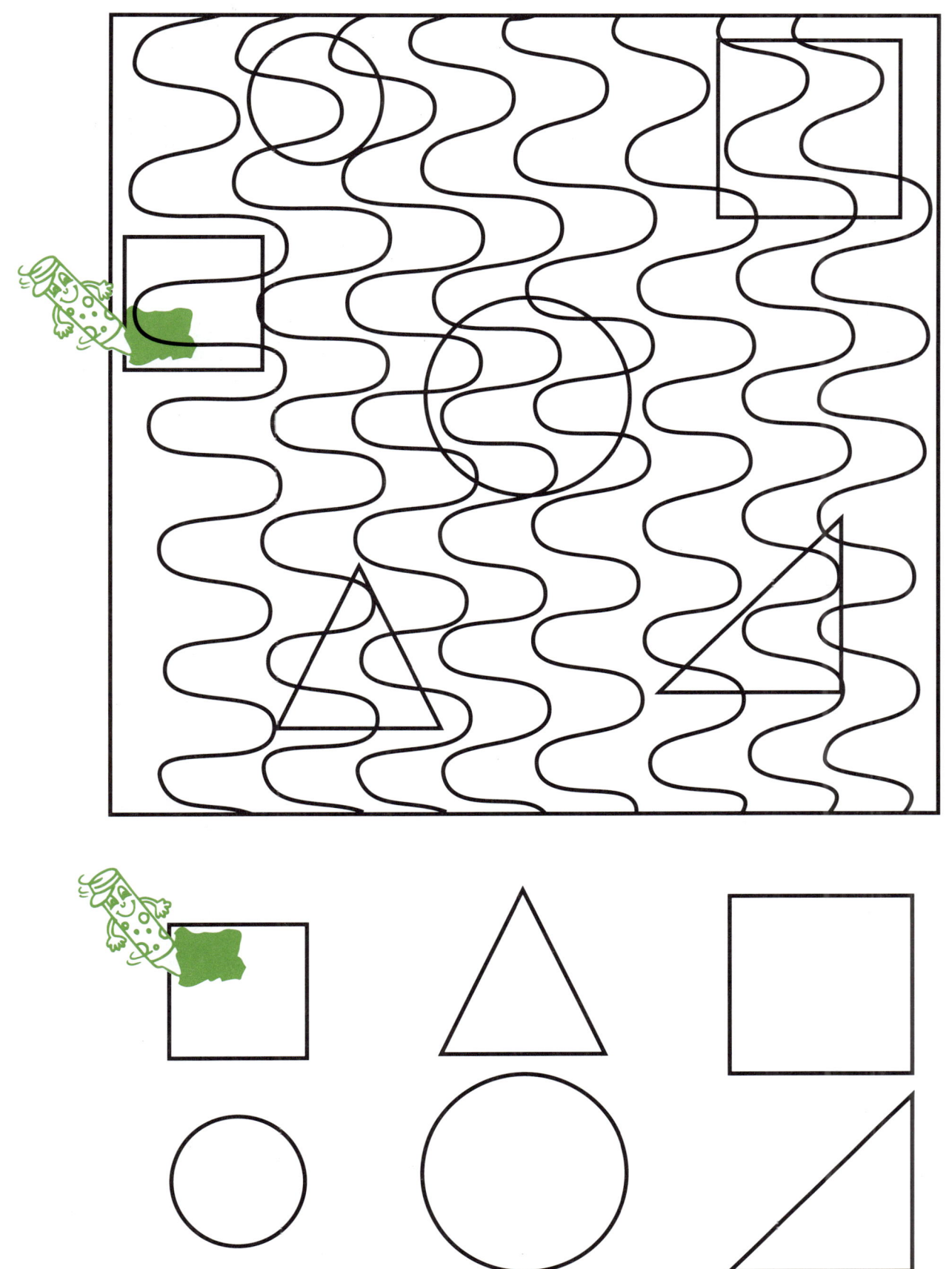

Find the shape

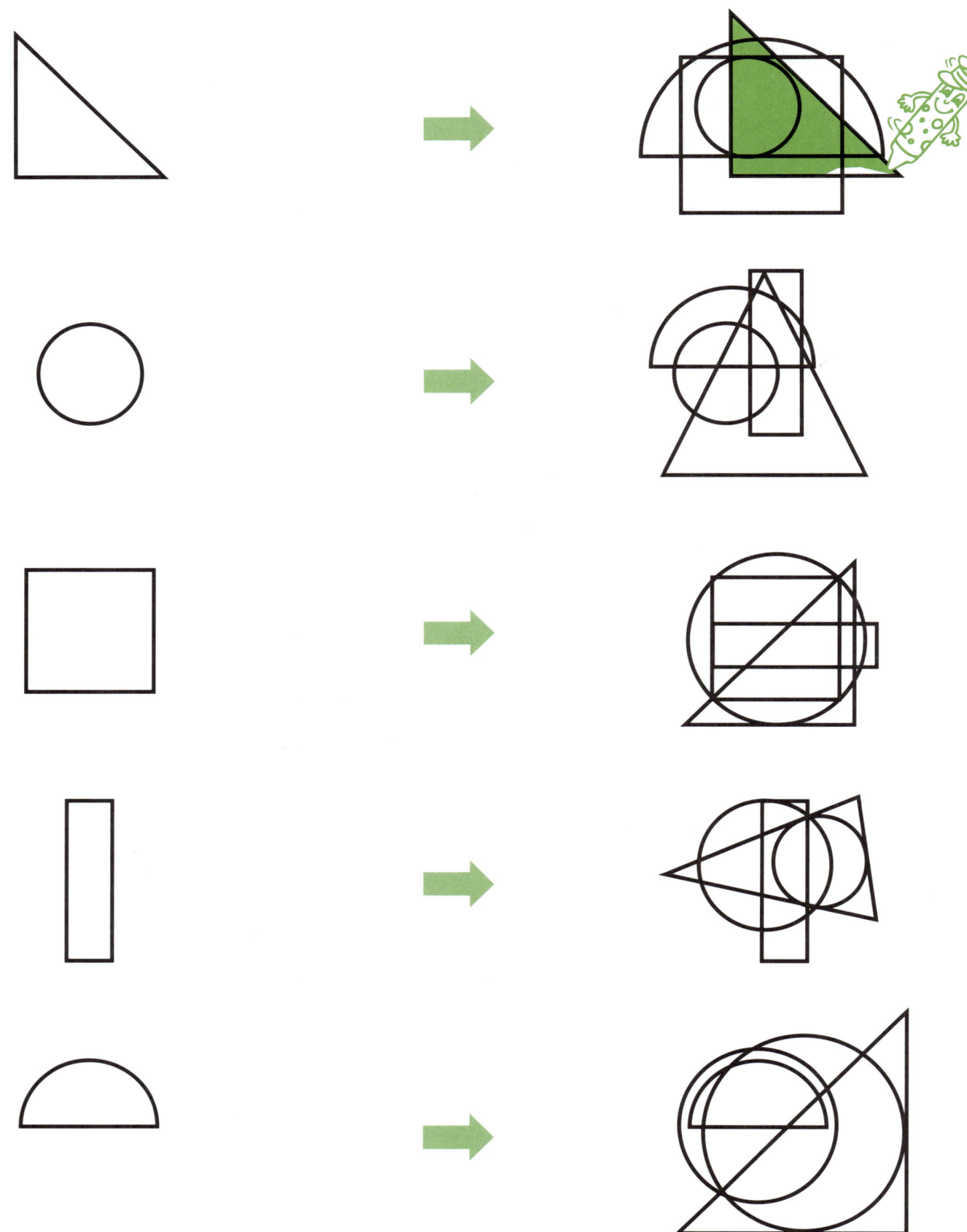

Find the shape

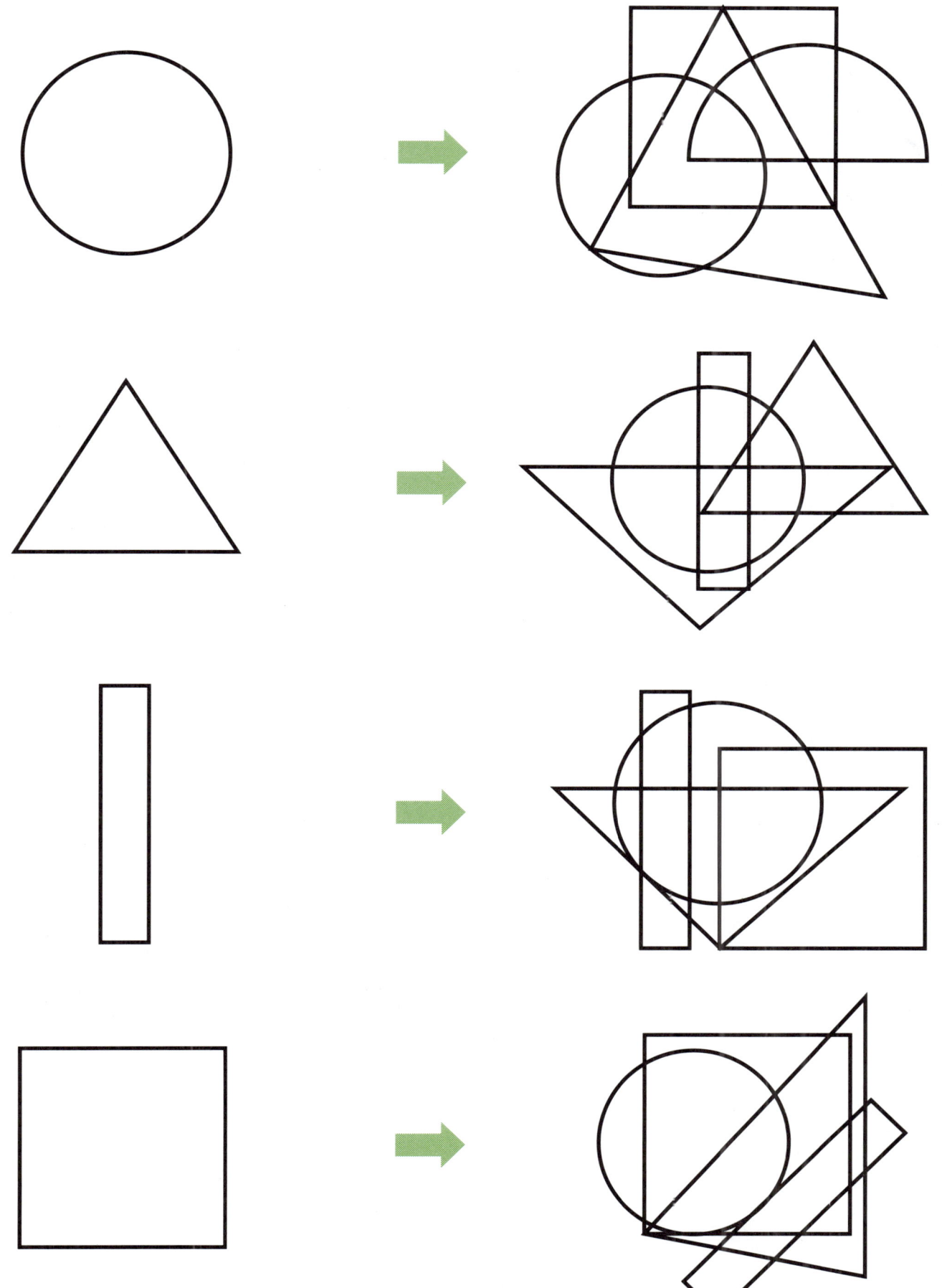

Colour the same size the same colour

blue red green

Colour the same size the same colour

purple pink black

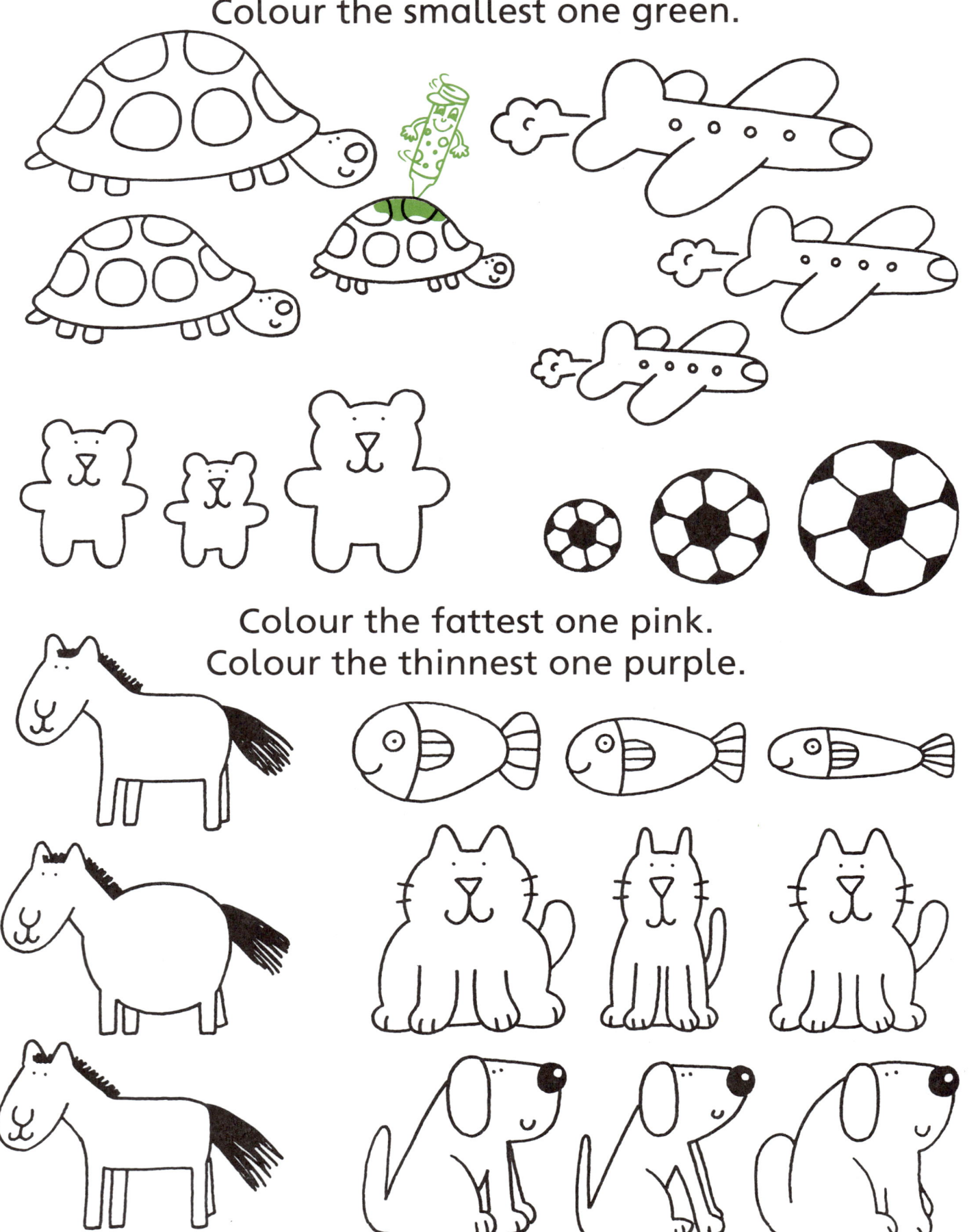

Colour the biggest one red.
Colour the smallest one green.

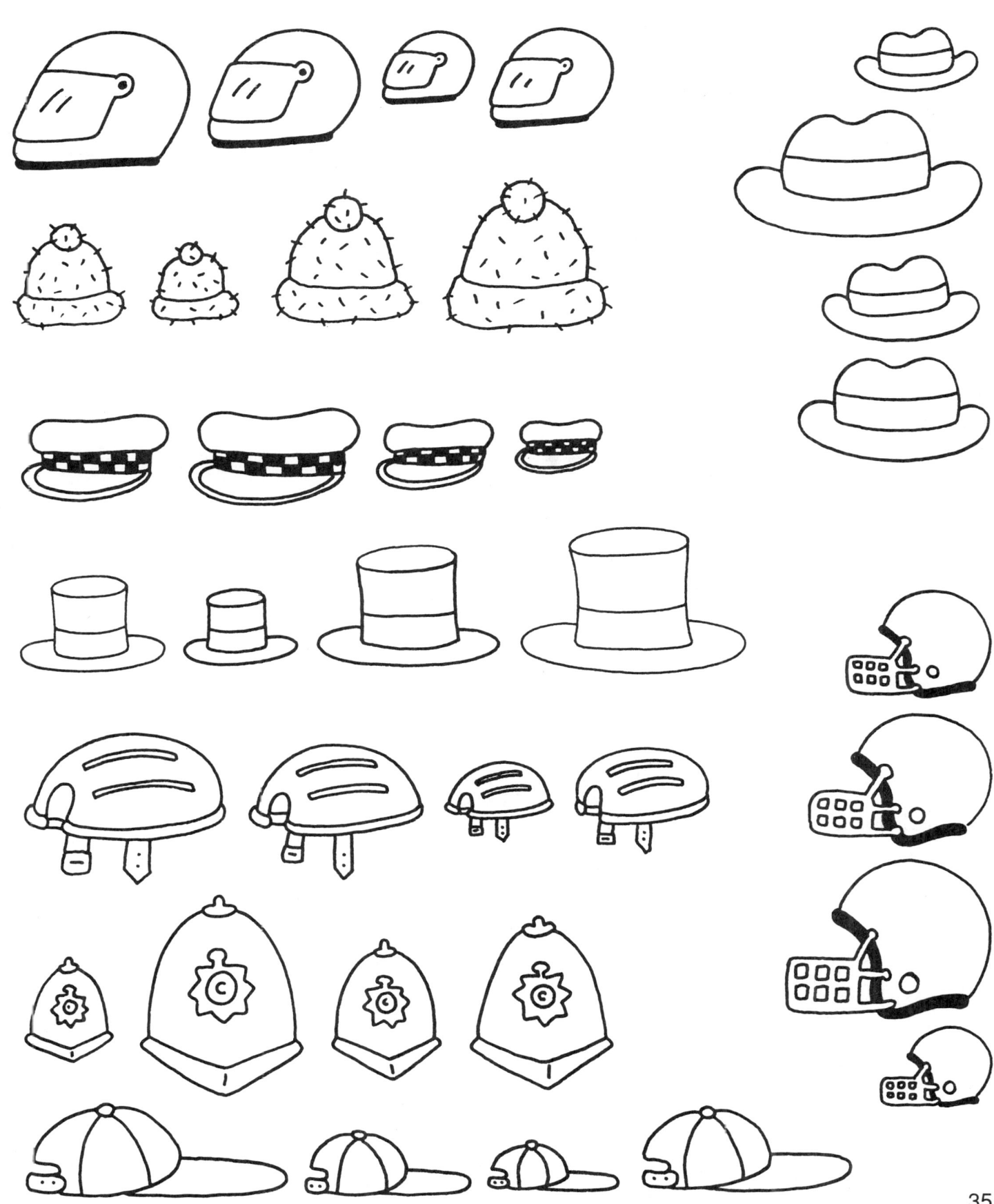

Colour the widest one green.
Colour the narrowest one black.

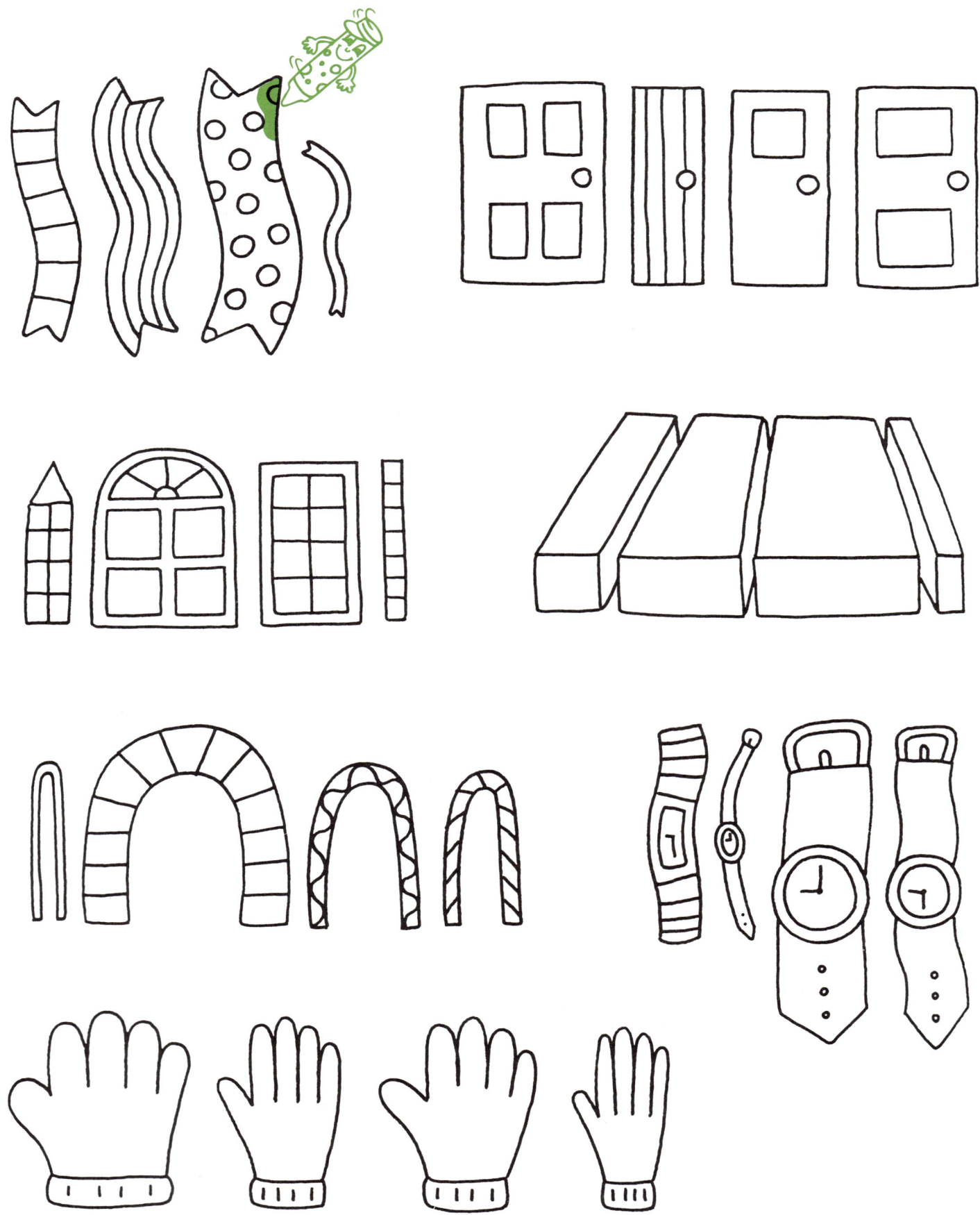

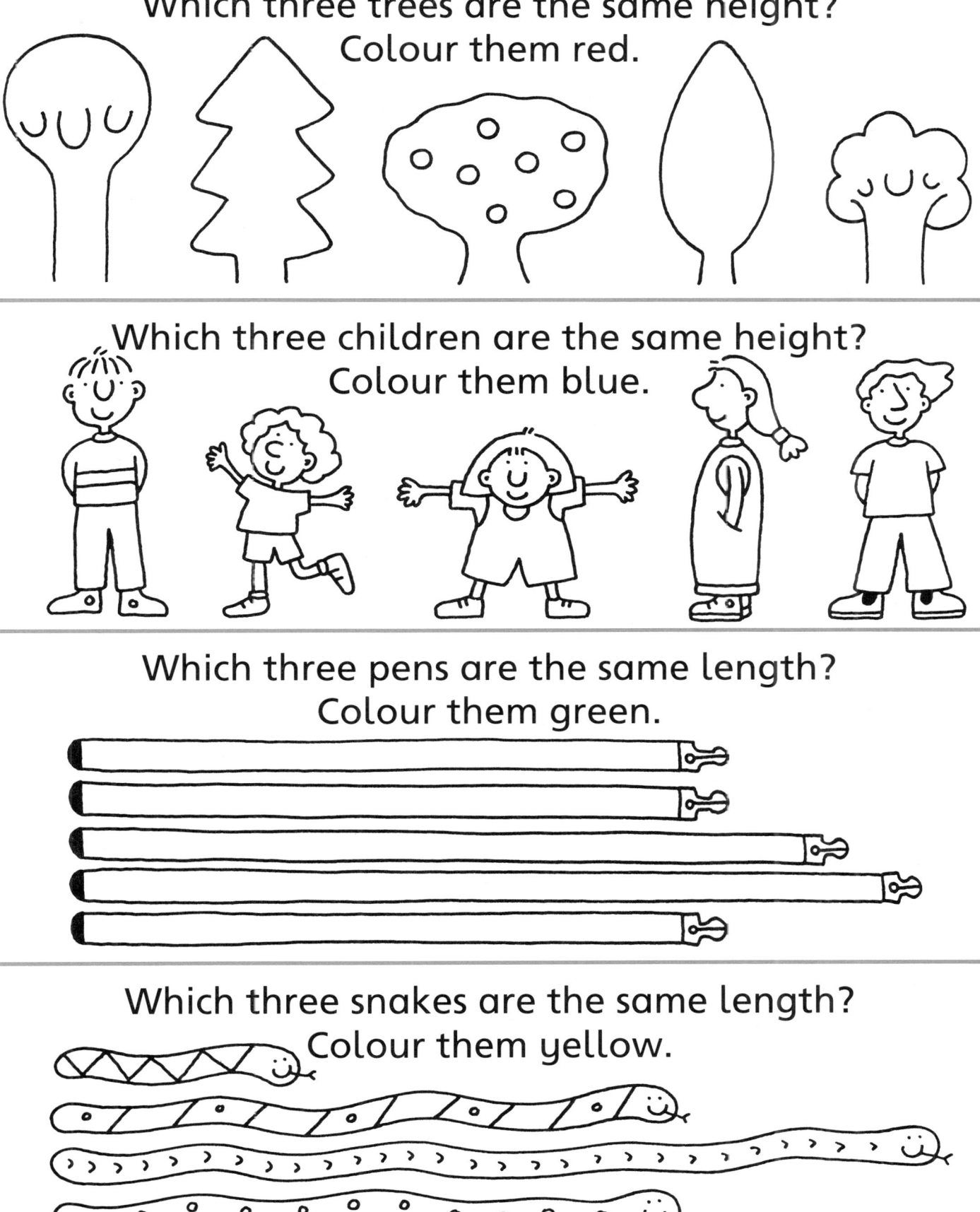

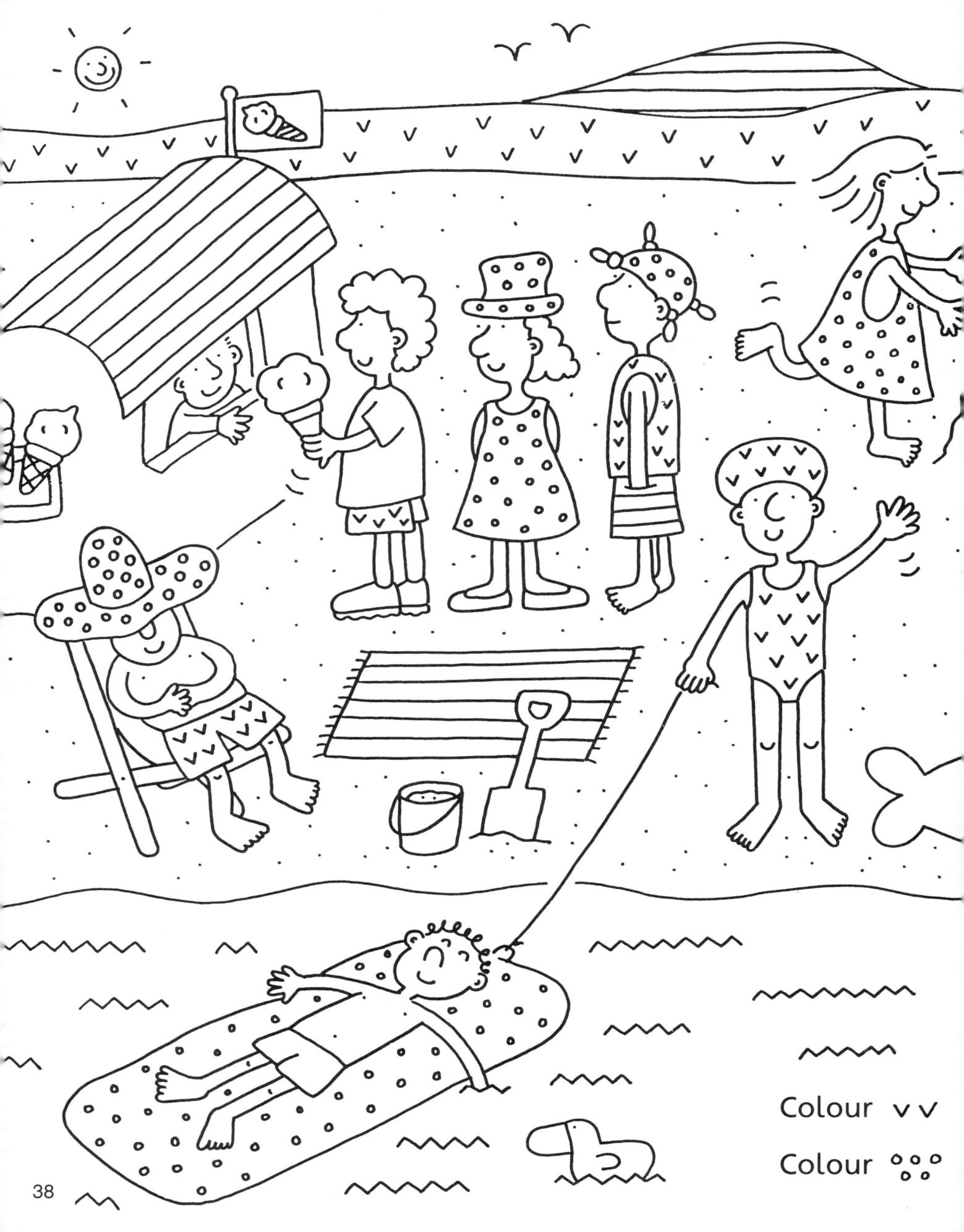

Colour ∨∨
Colour °°°

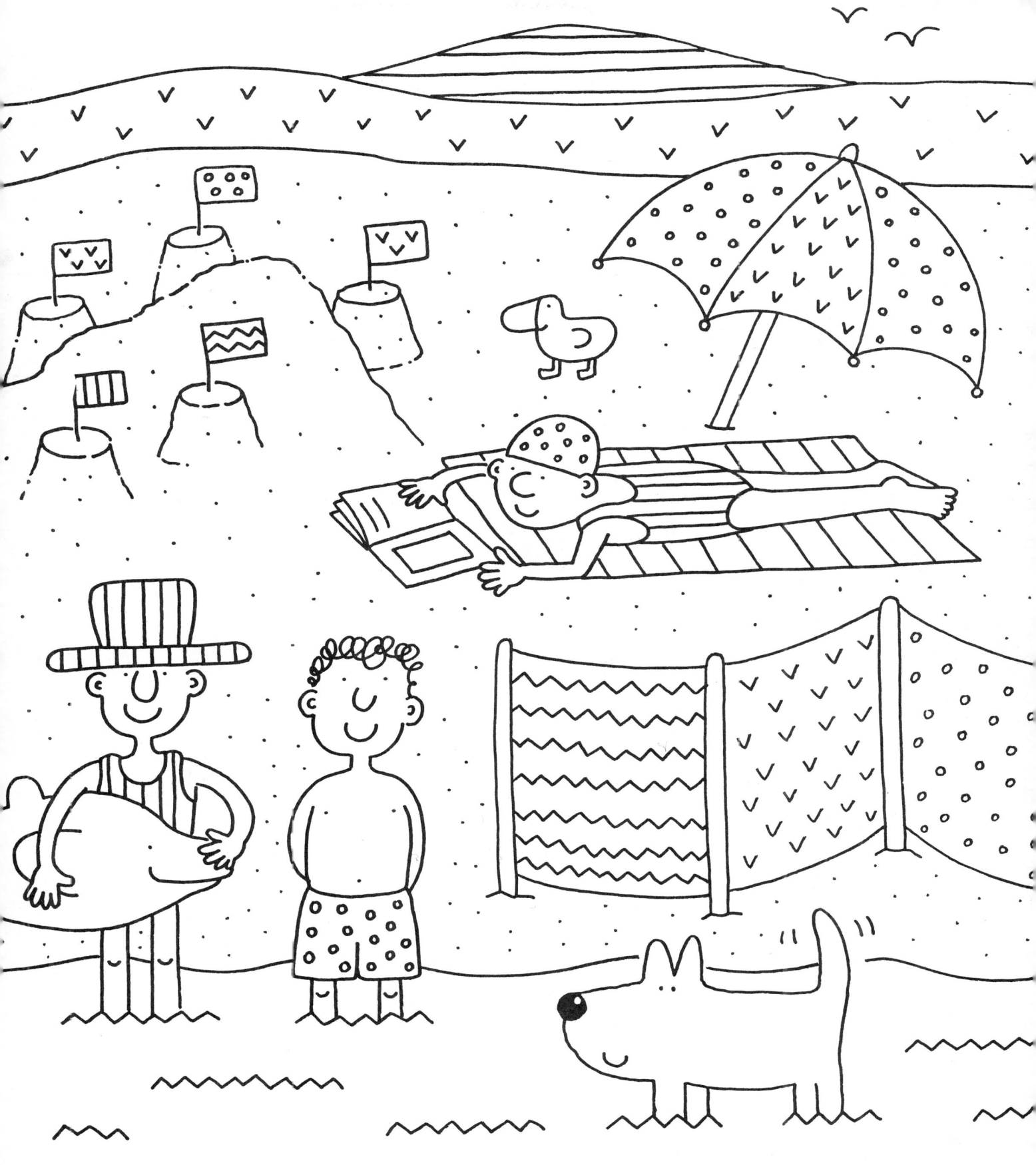

shapes green   Colour ∧∧ shapes blue

shapes red   Colour ≡ shapes yellow

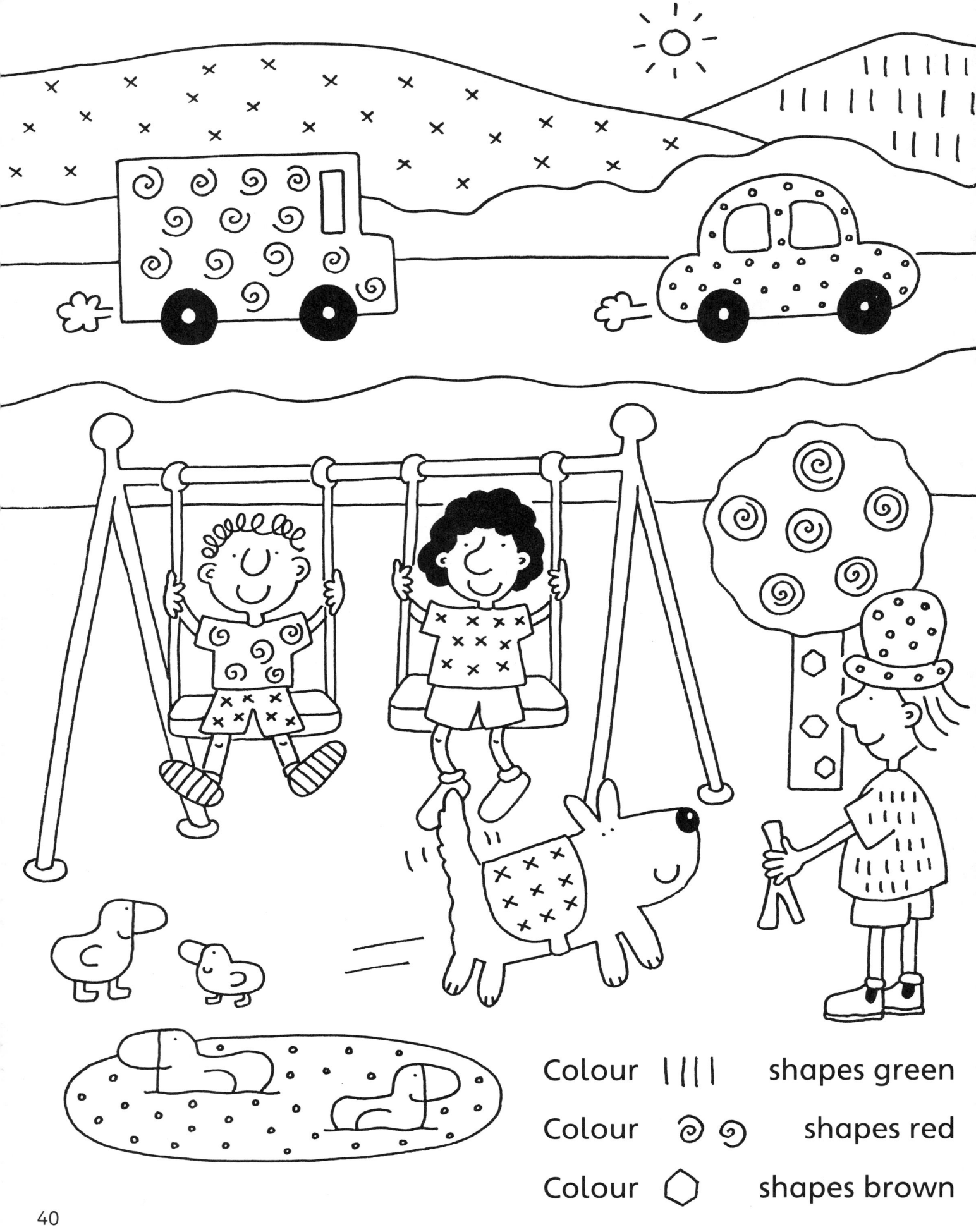

Colour |||| shapes green

Colour ⊙ ⊙   shapes red

Colour ⬡   shapes brown

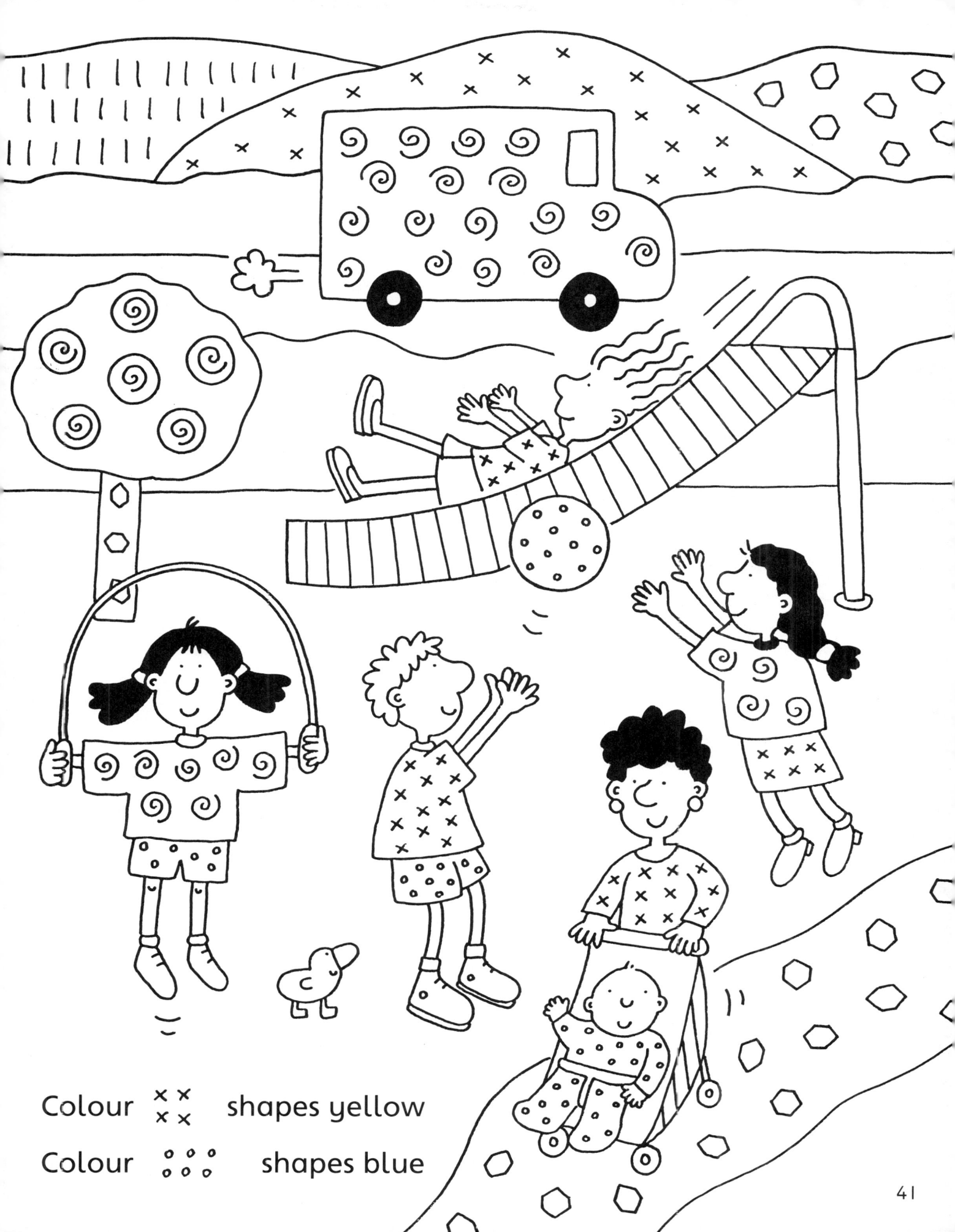

Colour ××/×× shapes yellow

Colour ∘∘∘/∘∘∘ shapes blue

41

What comes next?

What comes next?

What comes next?

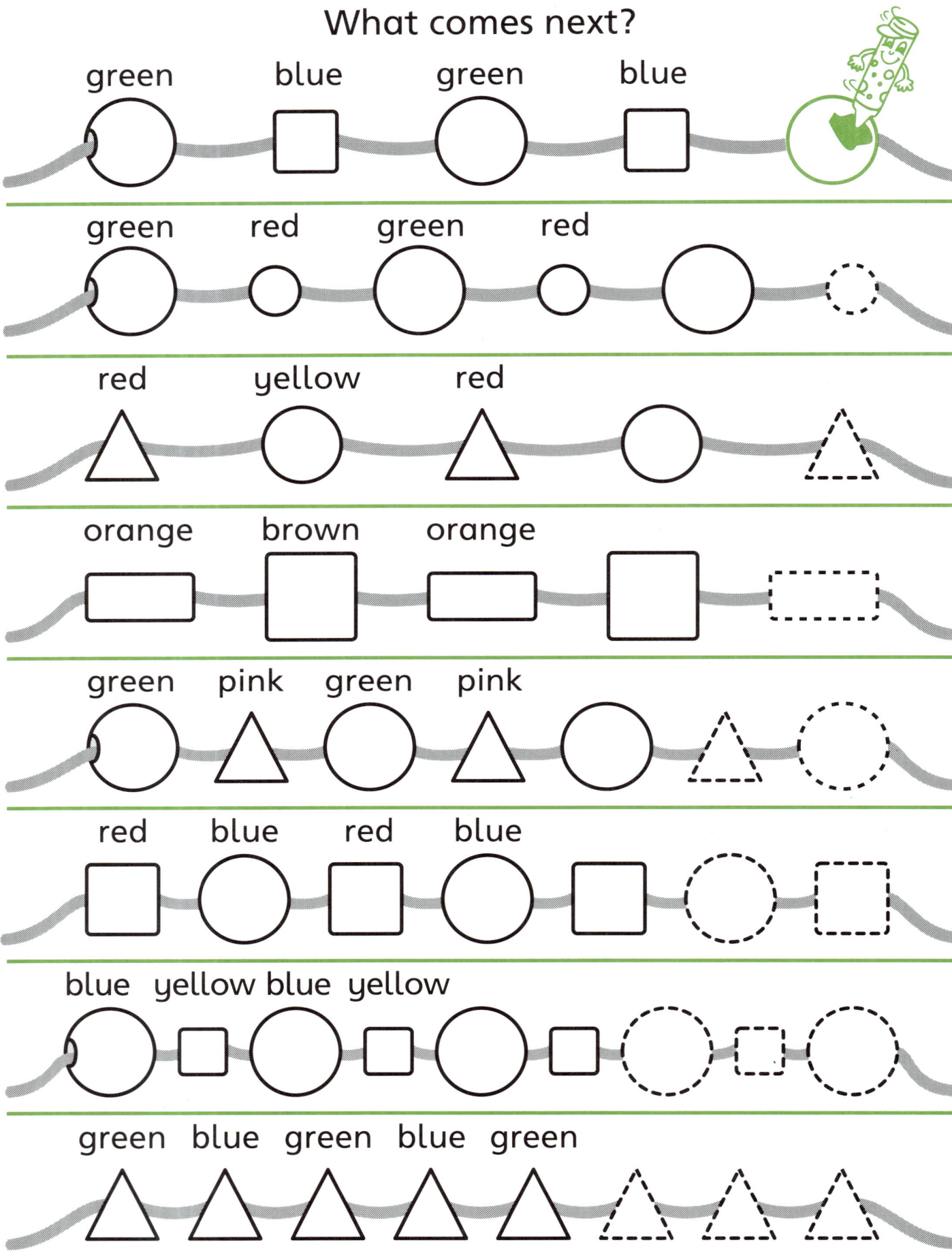

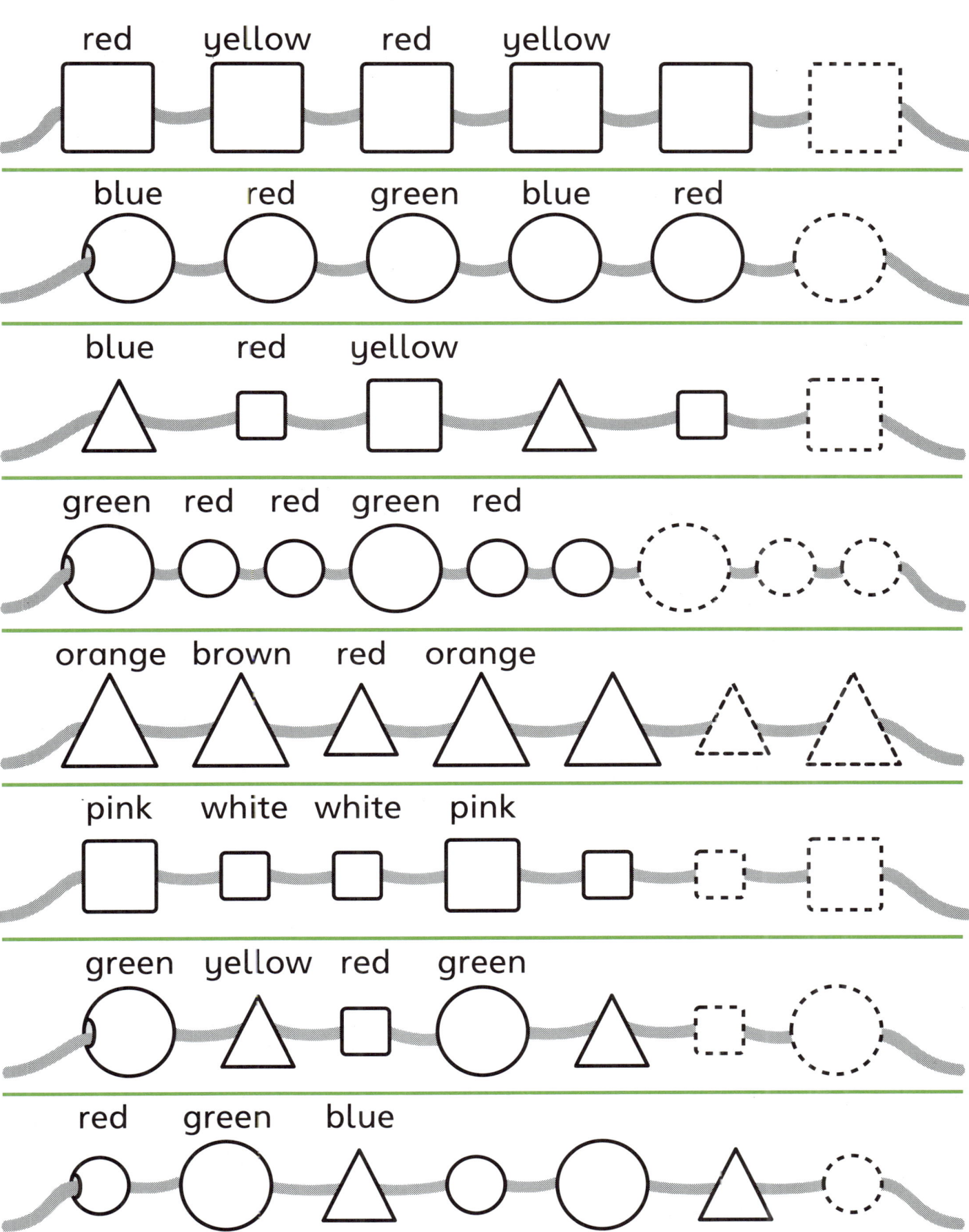

What comes next? Number the pictures.

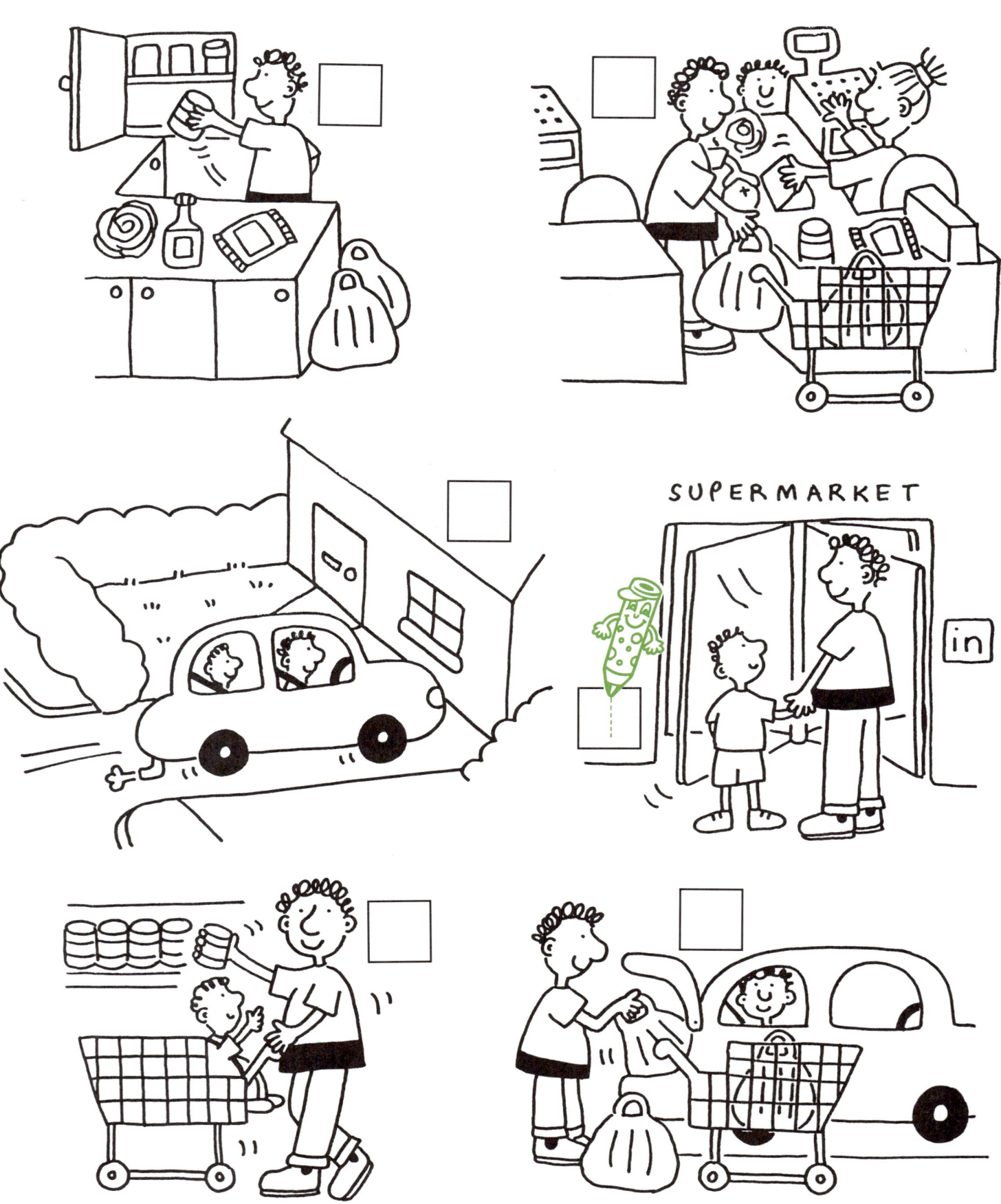

What comes next? Number the pictures.

47

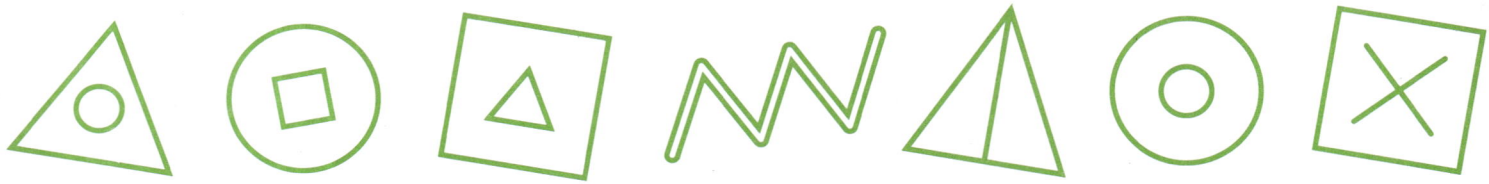

Notes for parents

Join the same pp. 4–9   This section helps the child to identify and recognize similarities of shape and pattern. Parents can use the opportunity to discuss and compare the differences between objects around the home.

Find more the same pp. 10–13   As a progression from the previous workbook, the child now looks for three more identical patterns. It would be a good time to compare the positions of the shapes, lines and patterns; e.g. on p. 10 talking about what the animals and children are doing helps the child to describe the relative position of objects.

Make the same pp. 14–25   These pages help the child to compare position, length, shape, direction and flow. Early reference skills are introduced, e.g. on pp. 22, 23, 24 the child refers to a "key" to complete the task.

Find the shape pp. 26–31   This section is about recognizing common shapes and being able to identify them within a combination of superimposed shapes. It will help develop general perception skills, which are also relevant to "reading for meaning", when a child searches out essential information within a more complex presentation.

Same size pp. 32–33   An awareness of varying sizes is an important early perceptual skill. Many early Number concepts also rely on the child being able to make these comparisons and assessments of scale.

Biggest and smallest pp. 34–37   This follows on from the previous section and further develops the child's skills of comparison.

Patterns pp. 38–41   Pattern in mathematics is not about decoration, but about repetition and sequencing. These two double-page pictures encourage perceptual development, and good observational techniques. If the child can notice and retain patterns, similarities, and differences, this will build a firm foundation for awareness of shape and space.

What comes next? pp. 42–47   The child now develops his or her observational skills into making predictions. This also encourages the vital skills of reasoning and logical thought.

Oxford University Press
Great Clarendon Street, Oxford OX2 6DP

Oxford New York
Athens Auckland Bangkok Bogotá Buenos Aires
Calcutta Cape Town Chennai Dar es Salaam
Delhi Florence Hong Kong Istanbul Karachi
Kuala Lumpur Madrid Melbourne Mexico City
Mumbai Nairobi Paris São Paulo Singapore
Taipei Tokyo Toronto Warsaw

and associated companies in
Berlin Ibadan

Oxford is a trade mark of Oxford University Press

© Jenny Ackland 1994
First published 1994
Reprinted 1996, 1997, 1998, 1999, 2000

ISBN 0 19 838131 X

Designed by Oxprint Ltd, Oxford
Illustrations by Sue Cony
Printed in China

All rights reserved. No part of this publication may be reproduced, stored in a retrieval system, or transmitted, in any form or by any means, without the prior permission in writing of Oxford University Press. Within the U.K., exceptions are allowed in respect of any fair dealing for the purpose of research or private study, or criticism or review, as permitted under the Copyright, Designs and Patents Act, 1988, or in the case of reprographic reproduction in accordance with the terms of licences issued by the Copyright Licensing Agency. Enquiries concerning reproduction outside those terms and in other countries should be sent to the Rights Department, Oxford University Press, at the address above.